How To Analyze People To Improve Your Life: Improve Your Emotional Intelligence, Understand Personality Types (Enneagram), Master Body Language & Protect Against Dark Psychology

© Copyright 2021 - All rights reserved.

The content contained within this book may not be reproduced, duplicated or transmitted without direct written permission from the author or the publisher.

Under no circumstances will any blame or legal responsibility be held against the publisher, or author, for any damages, reparation, or monetary loss due to the information contained within this book; either directly or indirectly.

Legal Notice:
This book is copyright protected. This book is only for personal use. You cannot amend, distribute, sell, use, quote or paraphrase any part, or the content within this book, without the consent of the author or publisher.

Disclaimer Notice:
Please note the information contained within this document is for educational and entertainment purposes only. All effort has been executed to present accurate, up to date, and reliable, complete information. No warranties of any kind are declared or implied. Readers acknowledge that the author is not engaging in the rendering of legal, financial, medical or professional advice.

Table of Contents

Introduction 10
What this book can do for you 11
The Link Between The Brain and Body Language Communication 13
How does the brain read body language? 15
Communication is the key to unlocking your ability to read people 16

Section One: Analyzing And Reading People Fast 17

Chapter 01: The Science Behind Analyzing People 18
Is there such a thing as mind-reading? 19
It starts with communication 21
    If you want to read and analyze people better, you need to become a masterful communicator. 22
Elements of any effective communication 23
How to analyze people 26
    To gain mastery of this skill, you'll have to do the following: 27
Importance of analyzing people 34
Can anyone speed-read people? 36

Advanced techniques to become a good speed reader 38

Chapter 02: Verbal and Non-verbal language. 41

What is verbal communication? 41

How tone can communicate the unspoken thoughts 42

Understanding non-verbal communication........... 44

    Types of non-verbal communication 45

The power of non-verbal communication............. 54

How body language is communicating different moods.. 56

Men and women differ in their non-verbal communication. 58

Am I in control of my body language? 58

Body language changes depending on a person's intentions... 61

Chapter 03: Body Language 64

Why is Body language so important in our lives? 66

The science of body language............................... 67

The East and The West Differ 69

Chapter 04: Body Language Cues And Meanings 71

Body cues and what they signal............................ 73

    Open body language examples 74

    Closed body language examples....................... 79

Hand gestures 82
Body movements 87
    Decoding the mouth: 89
    What the eyes can tell you: 90
    Breathing Clues 91
    Arms: 92
    Legs and feet: 93
Context and Culture 94
    How culture influences non-verbal communication 94

Section Two: Psychology and Personality Types 98

Chapter 05: What Is Psychology And Why Does It Matter? 99

A little more on Psychology and how it evolved: 100

Importance of psychology when reading people 103

How behaviors develop 104

    Factors that affect behavior 106

Can you determine behavior from communication style? 107

    Assertive behavior 107

    Aggressive behavior 108

    Passive behavior 109

    Passive-Aggressive behavior 110

Manipulative behavior 111
Positive psychology and dark psychology: what's the difference? 111

Chapter 06: Personality Types 113

What is personality? 113

What makes up a personality? 114

Personality Vs. Character 115

The spectrum of all personality types and personality traits 117

Personality Types in detail 122

Reading personality types.................................. 129

How to tell a person's personality type fast 133

Understanding what drives people...................... 135

Rules to help you read others: 139

One. I assume that everyone cares more about themselves than me... 140

Two. People are almost always driven by selfish altruism. 141

Three. Thinking isn't a commonplace activity, so don't assume the other person is actively thinking about each and every non-verbal signal. 143

Four. Conformity is the standard operating system. 143

Manipulative personalities (The dark triad) 145

Chapter 07: Non-verbal Cues For Deception. 149

Why do people lie? 149

How to spot a liar 153

Chapter 08: The Enneagram Personality Typing 156

The Enneagram Symbol 157

How the Enneagram Works 158

The Nine Enneagram Type Descriptions 159

    Type 1: The Reformer 159

    Type 2: The Helper 163

    Type 03: The Achiever 166

    Type 4: The Individualist 170

    Type 5: The Investigator 174

    Type 6: The Loyalist 177

    Type 7: The Enthusiast 181

    Type 8: The Challenger 185

    Type 9: The Peacemaker 189

Section Three: Emotional Intelligence Quotient 193

Chapter 09: Introduction To Emotional Intelligence 194

EQ versus IQ 195

How to cultivate your EI 196

Chapter 10: Different Emotions And Different Signals 200

The basic theory of emotions 201

A deeper look at microexpressions: 202
Emotions and their interpretations 203
    Happiness 203
    Surprise 204
    Fear 205
    Anger 206
    Disgust 208
    Sadness 209
    Signs of Interest 210
    Signs of Annoyance and irritation 211
    Signs of Shame 212
    Signs of Confusion or perplexity 212

Section Four: Tying It All Together 214

Chapter 11: Understanding People 215

Communication styles 218

Chapter 12: Speed Reading And Analyzing People In The Workplace 225

Three techniques that will help you in the workplace: 228

    Exercise: 230

Chapter 13: How To Date Or Befriend People With Complex Personalities 231

Listen and trust your instincts 233

Simple secrets to getting along with anyone 234

Chapter 14: Tips For Influencing Anyone 237
Mirroring.. 239
Empathy 241
Conclusion 244
Resources 247

Introduction

Have you ever walked into a room full of people and felt a sudden rush of excitement in your body? Perhaps that made you nervous, and you started freaking out because you could not accurately interpret what to expect from the eyes glaring at you. Someone more skilled at reading and analyzing people would have had a different experience. Instead of panicking, he would confidently move across the room, interact with just the right people, and come away feeling satisfied and perhaps with the exact outcome he desired. Throughout history, we've seen how charismatic, effective communicators can walk into a room and win the hearts of everyone they desire. Success seems inevitable for the few individuals who have mastered this art of reading, understanding, and effectively communicating with different personality types. Would you like to join the ranks of such individuals? Have you decided to reach for success and improve your chances of getting your way in life? If your answer is a resounding yes, then congratulations, you're in the right place. You now hold in your hand a communication bible that will unlock the dormant potential you've had all along of being a masterful communicator and influencer.

You see, the secret to getting ahead in life, especially in today's society, isn't about physical appearance, in-born talent, feats of strength, or extraordinary intelligence. Take a look around you. How many average joes do you see rising into stardom, fame, fortune, and success? They don't have anything more special than you. Many of the rags-to-riches stories that fill social media today prove that success in life has very little to do with the myths we were taught as kids and, instead, everything to do with the art of understanding and reading people better. So if you can learn to masterfully analyze, connect with and influence people in the right way, you can carve out whatever future you desire.

What this book can do for you

This book doesn't profess to teach whimsical or magical solutions that will work instantly, but it will give you lasting principles that will have people eating out of the palm of your hand when applied over time. And by people, I mean all kinds of varying personalities, including people you've struggled to get along with in the past. Remember that old boss you couldn't get to promote you or even like you no matter how hard you tried? Perhaps for you, it was a horrid experience of having the woman of your dreams reject you over and over again! Maybe your case is special, and you've spent your entire life as an introvert because understanding humans was a subject too confusing to explore. I don't know why you picked up this book, but I'm sure there's a pressing reason behind it. And even if it's just out of sheer curiosity, I want to encourage you to suspend all your existing beliefs, switch on your beginner's mind, and allow this book to guide you into a better version of yourself.

The topic of human behavior, personalities, body language, and how we communicate with each other has always fascinated me. Maybe it's because I struggled to read into people's emotions, intentions, and actions as a kid. I always felt disconnected from most of my relationships except for my mom. That was a very frustrating childhood, and as soon as I got the chance to study psychology, I decided to devote all my time to understanding human behavior and relationships. What makes us tick? How can we develop deeper connections and trust? Is influence real? How do we influence each other, and best of all, how can we tell what someone is trying to communicate even before they utter a word? These have always been fascinating questions for me, and if you've needed a simple guide that provides these answers, I invite you to join me on this journey of self-mastery and understanding of others.

As human beings, we've evolved significantly in the last two hundred thousand years. And in all that time, we've perfected interacting with each other and the world in various ways. Through the use of our physical senses, we've found ways of interpreting the world around us and each other. Some do it better than others, but all do it in their daily interactions. Did you know you're constantly reading, analyzing, and interpreting your environment and the people around you? It might not be as detailed or epic as Sherlock Holmes, but you still do it. Think for a moment about this scenario.

You're rushing home late evening as dusk turns into night, and you find yourself in a dark part of the alley. The dim lights and the darkening night sky make all human figures a blur. Walking right toward you is the figure of a man, and at first, you cannot make out who this person is or why they seem to be headed right toward you. In an instant, your brain goes into overdrive, attempting to read and analyze the situation. Are you in danger? Is this male figure a friend or a threat? How should you proceed? Within a matter of seconds, you'll make up your mind and act in a specific way (even if it means standing still in a panic). If you're able to identify this male figure as your friend quickly, your body will immediately relax, and you'll continue moving toward the person to greet them. If, in contrast, you read something life-threatening into the situation, you'll go into fight, flight, or freeze mode, depending on your personality type.

The point is, you just had an experience analyzing people. So this book isn't teaching you some magical capability that you don't yet have, but instead, it's here to enhance those powers so you can use them anytime, anywhere to your advantage. The best starting point is always the beginning.

The Link Between The Brain and Body Language Communication

In our case, the beginning seems to be the connection between the brain and the body. Did you know your body constantly communicates? If I'm standing or sitting across from you in a Starbucks coffee shop and we're chatting up about my book and how it helped you, I would be paying attention to both your words and your body. If what you say and the signals your body sends me align, my receptors would feel a certain harmonious vibe coming from you. I would then perceive you as confident, genuine, and overall a nice person who makes me feel good about my work. If, however, there was an incongruence between your words and body language, I would intuitively and subconsciously pick this signal up. Something would feel "off" for me, and since I am well versed in analyzing body language, I would be able to identify why you felt "off" during our interaction.

Now imagine how cool it would be if you awakened this same capability? It turns out, in order to activate this superpower, you just need to head over to your brain.

Interacting with other people requires both verbal and non-verbal communication, with information being processed in parallel. When we speak of non-verbal (which you'll learn about a lot in this book), we mean body language and the different movements that come with that. Although we rely heavily on verbal communication, it's crucial to understand body language because experts say more than 50% of our communication is based on body language. Through body language, we can infer and interpret feelings and intentions better. Analyzing people is, therefore, pretty hard if you don't know how to read body language. At first, one might assume reading another's body language is pretty easy because you just need to observe their movements, gestures, and body postures. But the process is actually highly complex. It involves specific regions and complex neural networks in our brains to decode body expressions and assign the appropriate meaning.

How does the brain read body language?

Scientific literature suggests that we have several specialized structures in our brains that process socially relevant information. Neuroimaging studies reveal that the processing of body expressions activates a complex network of neurons. This includes visual areas such as subcortical and cortical emotion-related regions and regions involved in planning and executing actions. So we know for sure that certain brain areas are always activated in order to process body language and facial expressions. Among these, two visual regions, as well as the amygdala, are the most important. Depending on gender and other personality-related factors, we may react differently to certain body language. In the second section of this book, we'll dive deeper into different personality types and how you can get better at analyzing and reading diverse personalities fast. Although your brain is getting a crash course on how to do it right, always bear in mind that understanding humans cannot be a one-size-fits-all approach because each human is unique. A person's childhood, personality type, attitude, character, and environment all play a significant role in who they become and how they behave in life, so you always need to give yourself enough time for your brain to collect comprehensive data before making conclusions.

Communication is the key to unlocking your ability to read people.

Communication is a technique that many consider art, and rightfully so. None of us are born talking and spend the first few years of our lives making no sense whatsoever except to our moms. With time, guidance, and skill development, we learn to express ourselves. Unfortunately, most of us stop developing this skill which creates a hindrance as we grow older. If done well, communication will help you excel in almost every area of yourself, and in contrast, it can also become a huge hindrance and disruptor. Since communication is basically the only way to transfer information between individuals, it's critical to the health of your career, relationships, and your ability to persuade and influence people. So even as we train you into the art of analyzing others, realize that this is all part of making you a masterful communicator. You need to continue developing all the elements of a masterful communicator, including your listening and observational skills.

Section One: Analyzing And Reading People Fast

Chapter 01: The Science Behind Analyzing People

Any big problem you can think of in your life has "poor communication and poor relationship" at its core. Family and personal relationships fall apart because of ineffective communication. Businesses often struggle and fail because senior leadership disconnects with the rest of the employees and makes it impossible to evoke the best from their people. Despite our advancement with technology and communication tools, we find it harder and harder to connect with each other. When there's no connection, there will be no trust, and where trust lacks, no lasting relationship can form. The solution to this problem is to develop the necessary skills to read, analyze, and communicate with people more effectively. That's what this section is going to walk you through. You need to learn what makes people tick and how to influence their behaviors.

Can you really analyze people from their body language or the way they behave?
Most of us have experienced moments in life when words seem to run away. Perhaps we got too nervous, too shy, too overwhelmed by emotions, or experienced some combination of these states, preventing us from speaking clearly. Regardless, I'm sure there was a time in life when all you could do

was utilize your body to convey a message. That's an example of how powerful body language can be. Even without words, we can observe and understand (if expressed accurately) what the person is attempting to say even if they don't utter a single word. The only barrier to analyzing people through their body language is your ability to interpret what they are saying. Suppose you have the right frame of mind, high emotional intelligence, and enough skillset to read into their movements, behavior, and gestures. In that case, you can pretty much analyze and interpret anyone regardless of the words they speak. Therefore, I cannot emphasize enough the importance of setting yourself up for success by developing the right mindset with filters that enable you to become a good people analyzer. That means you must be aware of your own biases, beliefs, and assumptions regarding the people around you. But more on mindset a little later.

Is there such a thing as mind-reading?

That has become a commonly asked question, especially since more articles, books, and programs are circulating online on mind reading. If you're wondering whether you need to become a mind reader to analyze people, let me put that thought to rest. You don't need to become some kind of a *ninja* mind reader for you to understand what people convey through their body language. In the past, mind reading was associated with supernatural powers. It was considered something only certain individuals could do, but lately, science has been investing in solidifying mind reading as a scientific procedure. According to Scientific American, experimental research destined to enter medical practice shows that in just a few minutes of monitoring electrical activity in your brain using EEG and other methods, a doctor can reveal not only neurological illness but also mental conditions like ADHD and schizophrenia.

What's more, five minutes of monitoring electrical activity flowing through your brain while you do nothing but let your mind wander can reveal how your brain is wired. Tapping into this wandering mind can measure your IQ, identify cognitive strengths and weaknesses, discern your personality, and discover your aptitude for learning specific types of information. Of course, scientists being armed with this kind of ability is a fantastic proposition as long as they use it for good. For example, they can know what the person is thinking and what that person intends to do. So, a scientist could tell if a person is contemplating suicide simply by watching how the person's brain responds to words like "death" or "happiness." That, of course, can be a fantastic brain hacking technique used to save and prevent lots of bad things from happening. But with such great power comes great responsibility. The same scientific abilities make it possible to control the brain through electrical stimulation, and we all know how quickly that can go south in our society. All this is to point out that although science now proves that mind reading and mind control are real, you need not worry about it. It's still a highly complex process that most will never pull off. Unless, of course, they have some innate supernatural power or a very expensive lab. Your skillset for analyzing people will not focus on mind reading or mind control. To read, analyze, understand, and develop instant connections with other people, we're leveraging the best and most trusted technique that all human beings enjoy: active communication.

It starts with communication

Most people assume communication is simply talking. But the truth is, communication is the process of understanding others and being understood by others; it's a process of understanding and sharing meaning. This is usually achieved verbally, using your voice; visually, through images, maps, etc.; non-verbally, through body language, gestures, eye contact, etc.; and through written forms of communication, such as this book you're reading. A huge aspect of good communication is listening. Active listening is one of the great secrets to employ for masterful communication. Most of us are very poor listeners, and we barely pay any active attention to those we interact with. That's why analyzing people and interpreting body language can feel so hard. Our current society is so focused on voicing opinions that hardly anyone prioritizes listening. So as part of your initiation into reading and analyzing different personalities and their body movements, you're going to learn how to become an active listener.

If you want to read and analyze people better, you need to become a masterful communicator.

How would you like to walk into any room and immediately get a read of the people in that room? How much of a confidence boost would that give you? Just imagine how different your life would be if you could positively influence people with precision and naturally boost your charisma. Wouldn't it be great if you could motivate others easily and consistently because you know how to tap into the driving motivations of those individuals? Well, it turns out, the better you become at communicating, the easier it will be to do everything we just highlighted and more.

Start by being 100% clear about the desired outcome of your interaction and communication whenever you engage with someone. Ordinary people have no idea what they want to get out of an interaction. Masterful communicators have a clear result in mind, even if it's just making the other person feel valued. They know exactly what results they want to obtain, making it easier for them to become aware of the other person's signals. Imagine you're sitting in your boss's office trying to get a promotion. If you have a clear result in mind, you'll be more attuned to the verbal and non-verbal signals he sends you. If you're skilled enough, you can pick up on the direction he's heading and even redirect his energy to where it suits you best. For example, if, as you're speaking, you read that he's likely to say you're not ready for a promotion, you can stall that final decision by saying something like, "Sir, I know you might think I'm not ready to head the department. But I promise that if you give me a chance and a little more time to prove to you my worth and work ethic, in six months, I can show that I am ready to become more than the head of sales." By analyzing him properly and then communicating the right thing in the right way, you could essentially get your boss to slow down and give you a shot.

Elements of any effective communication

Communication is a logical process that begins with the sender conveying a message of some sort and the receiver interpreting that message, after which feedback is often given. That means there are certain elements we need to recognize in every interaction, namely encoding, message, transmission medium, decoding, and feedback.

• Encoding
Encoding refers to the act of "packaging a message." That's usually the work of the sender. It involves creating the message and accurately presenting it so that the recipient can properly understand it. The

clearer and more concise the sender is about the message they are trying to convey, the easier it will be to encode it appropriately. The easier it will also be for the receiver to understand and interpret the message correctly. At this point, we need to be cognizant of the fact that the message is always expressed through both non-verbal and verbal cues. When these two forms match up, the package is received quickly; when there's a conflict, the package is not easily received, and poor communication results.

• Message
A message is information conveyed during a communication exchange. The sender determines the information, and great communicators excel at this part because they always have a clear purpose and message to communicate when interacting with someone. The clearer they are about the intended outcome, the easier it becomes to determine the nature of the message and the medium through which that message can be passed.

• Transmission medium
By transmission medium, we refer to the "vehicle" or channel used to communicate. It's always essential to ensure your message is sent through the proper channel so the right person can receive it in the right way. For example, Face-to-face, text messaging, phone calls, online messaging platforms, social media, and so on are all transmission mediums.

- Decoding

Once the sender transmits the message through the proper channels, the receiver will pick it up and decode it. Decoding involves deducing or deriving meaning from the message received. A well-encoded message increases the likelihood that the receiver will get the message as intended by the sender. If, however, the message was ambiguous and open to various interpretations, the receiver will deduce meaning based on their filters. Communication is only considered effective and successful when the intended message is received and appropriately decoded.

- Feedback

The only way to know whether communication has occurred between two people is through the use of feedback. This part of communication is usually the final validation that a message has been passed on and is often the beginning of a new conversation. For example, feedback is essential if you initiate a conversation on Slack with your team member to let them know that you've completed your part in an ongoing project. They should come back to you with a seal of approval letting you know that they've taken over, which will end that loop for you, or they might request you make a few amendments, which will then lead to further conversations. In all communications, it's important to know what feedback signals to look out for. Even if someone appears to be hearing what you're saying, they may not necessarily understand the instructions you've given. Appropriate feedback makes it possible for you to know with certainty that the message was well received and understood.

These are the main elements in communication. Of course, there's also the non-verbal aspect that's ever-present, especially in face-to-face communication, which is what we'll invest the rest of our time on. When it comes to analyzing people, we run these elements as the backdrop for our execution of reading and analyzing the messages people transmit during an interaction.

How to analyze people

Do you think that this book will be some kind of FBI or CIA training to give you some unheard-of ninja skills? I'm sorry to disappoint, but this is a down-to-earth guide teaching skills that even the most average of us can adopt to improve our communication skills. While becoming the next Sherlock Holmes is complex and nearly impossible for the average Joe, what you'll learn here are strategies that are simple enough to conduct on your own. You don't need to have mind-reading powers (although sometimes it does seem to others like you're a mind reader), and these strategies certainly don't give you any psychic abilities. Analyzing people is intended as a means to better understand and relate to others in your life. Whenever something intrigues you or piques your interest, you pause a little longer to pay attention and grasp the intended meaning. People-analysis is a deliberate and more meaningful way to interact with humans because it opens you to things most people miss. And that makes all the difference when you need to influence another person.

To analyze people, you'll need patience, a keen eye, and an active ear. Decoding someone is simple, but not easy, because human beings are complex emotional creatures. We are also very unique. The same person could send you plenty of mixed signals within a short timeframe. That's why you should always involve all your senses and become somewhat of a self-proclaimed investigator when conversing with people. One signal simply doesn't help you accurately read someone. You need clusters of cues and pointers, both verbal and non-verbal, to make a good analysis. Once you've gathered enough data from the person, you'll be better equipped to communicate with the person and adjust your mannerisms accordingly. As you'll learn, through the process of living and meeting people, not everyone is naturally warm and welcoming. Some people are very open and easy-going, while others are the exact opposite. Practicing the skill of people-analysis is almost like an art, and it equips you to handle different personalities and varying situations.

To gain mastery of this skill, you'll have to do the following:

First, establish a mental baseline.

That means you become a keen observer when conversing with a person. How does this individual act when they are calm and talking about something trivial? What about when they get nervous, bored, irritated, and so on? Do they stammer when nervous or scratch their head? Do they switch to a closed position by folding their arms when angry? What about their facial expressions and eye movements? All this data enables you to bring out and zero in on specific personality traits, which we'll talk more about later in the book. How a person behaves under stress, pressure, or in unpleasant situations gives you important data that enables you to interpret (and predict)their moves in future interactions, so always try to establish a baseline for any individual you wish to analyze.

The second thing you'll do is compare and contrast.

Once you've observed the person long enough, you should have a bearing on what the person's true personality is like. Does this person act the same way around you and everyone else, or are they two-faced? Ever sat down for a meal with someone who acted pleasant with you all evening, only to turn around and yell at the poor waitress who mixed up his order? Surely that person isn't as kind as they pretended to be. That's not to say it's bad when we behave differently depending on the environment and the person in front of us. I expect my girlfriend looks at her colleagues and guy friends differently than she looks at me. I don't expect her to walk into her office and give everyone a tight hug that lasts five seconds too long and smile from ear to ear when she sees her boss. But I do expect she will be cheerful, respectful, and friendly toward her colleagues. So take note of how someone reacts toward several people and jot down your findings. If your conclusions are pretty similar, then you're likely dealing with a specific personality type. If, however, you get mixed reactions and end up with a web of confusion, don't worry; just exercise a little patience, and pretty soon, you'll crack that person's true nature.

The next thing you'll do is identify personality cues.

This part is essential because personality and character play a huge role in people's analysis. Everyone has that rare behavioral trait in them. Dig a little deeper, and don't get stumped with the surface-level stuff they show you. Through careful observation, you'll be able to notice whether the person is an egoist, an introvert, an extrovert, and so on. The person might pretend to be calm and cool, yet, when they're infuriated, they just snap. Or they might pretend to be okay with certain news, yet, in their eyes, you can see anger brewing. Seek beneath the mask the person might be wearing and try to identify their real personality.

The other thing you want to do is identify the voice.

By this, I mean that you should know whether the person has a strong or loud voice. These two should never be confused. A strong voice might be soft but comes out as bold and dominant. One can be the loudest person in the room and yet the weakest in the group. When we say a "strong voice," we don't just mean verbal talk; it's about how one expresses themselves. In a strong voice, you can pick up high levels of confidence and self-assurance. How the individual uses their words and how they pronounce things can tell you a lot. You could be able to tell whether someone is feeling rushed, relaxed, panicked, and so on. Observing such qualities will give you a better sense of what's happening in another person's mind.

The last thing you need to start doing is practicing the mirror technique and identifying deviations.

We will discuss the mirror technique at length throughout the book. The mirror technique is proven to be an effective way to develop instant rapport with someone. In our case, we want to initiate this action by returning a smile when we see it in the other person. We also want to deliberately test out some behaviors to see if the other person will reciprocate. For example, if they are talking, show engagement and involvement so the other person can see how interested you are. If you're exhibiting enthusiasm, try coupling that with an appropriate, light touch and see if that electrifies the flow or repels it. Notice also if the person then reciprocates with a variation of your touch and enthusiasm.

As you observe their actions, try to spot any inconsistencies that arise during the interaction. Are their words matching their energy and actions? Something contradictory might be a stammer when they're concerned or hesitancy when they're responding to your questions. It could be that the person is telling you how much they enjoy your company, and yet, when you lean in closer, they move away and close themselves off. These are all small cues that signal there's more to them than meets the eye and that it's up to you to identify the truth.

Of course, this is just an overview of how the analysis is done and what the foundational things you need to learn are, but I think that, by now, you're starting to understand the simplicity of this process. It's about being patient, mindful, and heavily invested in understanding the person in front of you without biased opinions.

Any time you meet someone, pay attention to the following clues. Start systematically from their head, moving down to their feet. Notice their eye contact. The key to understanding what message their eyes are transmitting is to bring to bear the environment and context in which you're interacting with that person. For example, if you're sitting across a dinner table for a first blind date with a person who cannot take their eyes off you, that's likely a strong indication of romantic interest. On the other hand, if you're in the office and the person you're interviewing can't seem to get themselves to make even a little eye contact as you speak, it's probably a sign that they are incredibly nervous about something.

Next, you should pay attention to the eyebrows as they communicate a lot about the person's emotional state. Certain emotions (which we'll talk about later) cause the eyebrows to rise or fall in a particular way. You want to observe the smile and how the face crinkles (or doesn't) as the person smiles. While it's important to recognize these features, let's not forget to actively listen for the spoken words. What someone says and how they say it can help you quickly read a person's personality. For instance, if you meet someone for the first time and they can't stop raving about how great their boss, wife, husband, or colleagues are, chances are they are pretty decent themselves. But whenever you encounter a person with a sour look who can barely find something positive to say about the waitress serving you coffee, their ex-husband, or their boss, you're likely dealing with a very sour personality type. Studies show that the more people rate others as being kind, polite, loving, and well-mannered, the more likely they are to possess these traits. However, the reverse is also true. People who love backstabbing and describing others as manipulative and nasty are more likely to have these traits. Take note of the words people use to describe their friends, co-workers, and family members, as that gives you a base for personality analysis. That brings me to another key aspect of analysis: take notice of paralanguage, which involves the tone and manner in which one speaks.

As you continue to move from top to bottom with your observation, take note of the other person's glance. People who are open to meeting you and interested in that interaction tend to have their entire body facing in your direction. They also tend to look you in the eye. By contrast, a disinterested person will often look away, giving you a side glance. And just by paying attention to the direction of their body, you might notice it is oriented away from you. That is often a subconscious signal that indicates the person is subtly looking for an escape route.

How someone carries themselves and their overall body posture can help you figure out their confidence level, how calm or nervous they are, and so much more. We'll be talking more about the common body postures and hand gestures so you can have a library of different interpretations. That way, you can combine context with this newly acquired skill to make an informed conclusion about a person. You can also tell a lot about a person's handshake. Soft and floppy handshakes are generally associated with submissive people. Confident people tend to have firm handshakes, but they aren't too tough or crushing because that indicates extremism and authoritarian personalities. How long that handshake lasts can also tell you a lot. If someone grabs your hand and won't let go, that's pretty weird, don't you think?

But on the other hand, you don't want a squirmy and short handshake unless that person doesn't want to make a connection with you. Another thing to pay attention to is whether a person leans in toward you or away. If someone values you and wants to confide in you or show that they respect you, they'll often lean in as you interact, especially when you start discussing something important. Whenever you notice someone pulling back and away or sinking into their chair, it could be that they've just become uncomfortable or grown tired of the conversation. The same subtle signal can be observed with the feet. When someone likes you and wants to engage in conversation, they will likely have their feet pointed toward you. But when they are disinterested or seeking to escape that interaction, their toes and feet will be facing the door.

Importance of analyzing people

Analyzing people makes for easier relations with others. For instance, think about starting a new job at your dream company. Those first few days and weeks at the job matter a lot. The way people perceive you, especially those under you and those above you, will determine your overall experience and enjoyment of working at that new organization. Suppose you can communicate well with people and quickly learn to identify and handle the different personalities in the workplace with their varying dispositions, beliefs, and prejudices about the company. In that case, things will go smoothly for you. That's one of the key things about learning this art of effective communication and people analysis. You cannot get along with people without first having a familiar or common base to start with. You have to know what to portray, what not to portray, as well as when, where, and through what means. Not everyone will have the same reaction to your advances, confrontations, or even a mere friendly "hello." So when you can first analyze that person and get to know them and their personality, you'll develop a common ground for trust to blossom.

It's also beneficial to read others because you can quickly determine and understand their mental states. Mental health issues have become a real problem in our society. People today are more sensitive, and egos are pretty fragile, so you need to handle co-workers, strangers, and even friends differently. Understanding other people and their mental states will help you know what degree of attention or engagement to give. People's feelings tend to vary and shift as per social expectations or situations. Even the hard-headed boss will soften up if you play your cards right, so it's up to you to find pointers that will lead you to the highest and best solution for all parties concerned and then deploy appropriate handling techniques. The last section of this book will offer a variety of strategies and techniques for you to store in your communication toolbox, so don't worry about that for now. The most important takeaway for you is that developing the ability to read and analyze people will become a tool that will make it easier for you to work with, co-exist harmoniously with, and even influence whomever you choose. People are different. Some take everything personally and get easily offended; others shun and easily move on. Some are submissive, while others are overly aggressive and insecure. You will not always be everyone's cup of tea, no matter how hard you try to make everyone like you. But by identifying personalities and analyzing people the right way, even those who don't resonate with you will learn to respect you. That's the power of effectively analyzing people.

Can anyone speed-read people?

Speed reading is something we are all familiar with. The famous brain coach Jim Kwik has created entire programs to help people learn how to read one book a week. But that's not really what we're talking about here. In this context, we mean the ability to rapidly observe and analyze a person so you can get to know them better. Perhaps there is some similarity to speed reading a page on a book so you can get the gist of what the author is trying to communicate, but with humans, it's a tad bit more complex. Instead of taking lots of time to decode a person through character traits and behavior, you do a quick data collection of the most important things that will enable you to form an analysis. Speed reading people requires a very sharp and focused mind. You cannot undertake this activity if your mind is distracted by other things or if you haven't been practicing mindfulness. When speed reading, you're racing against time or resources. Usually, you only have limited access to one or both of these, and it's up to you to act quickly to achieve your desired outcome. That means you need an active mind with all your senses engaged. Speed reading and analysis also require critical thinking and a formula for identifying and discerning the data points that matter. Practice is key for this to work. That's why we never suggest this as a beginner's move. Consider this scenario: a young man is introduced to an attractive woman at a party, and he only has a few seconds of face-to-face contact to determine, discern, and interpret whether the woman is interested in getting a dinner invitation from him. In a matter of seconds, this young man has to process lots of information and come to a quick conclusion before he loses touch with the woman; otherwise, he may never get the right opportunity to ask her out. If he is distracted or unable to maintain sharp focus and speed-read her verbal and non-verbal cues, he won't stand a chance at making the right move that will get him the highest and best outcome. The young man must mentally compute all the data he receives, cross out the second-tier traits, and focus on the dominant cues that make more sense to ongoing activities.

We engage in some form of speed reading in our daily lives, although it's mainly at a subconscious level. Consider this scenario: You're walking down the street in the evening. You come across a suspicious-looking person, and what do you do? You take some form of action to protect yourself, of course. Now, pause and think for a moment about how you were able to conclude that you were in danger. That's called speed reading. In a fraction of a second, your brain analyzed bits of data such as the clothes the guy was wearing, how he walked, his body language, etc., and determined he could be a bad guy. Although your brain can do this and usually does it when safety and survival are concerned, you can get exponentially better by training yourself to become a powerful speed reader.

Advanced techniques to become a good speed reader

Although you need to begin your quest with the foundational stuff that rolls out in the upcoming chapters, let me just share a few advanced hacks that you can come back to once you've built a strong foundation for your communication techniques. Remember, most of these get better with practice.

• **A heightened ability to scan people.**

Think of a document scanner, and you'll know exactly what I mean by this. You scan a person with your eyes from top to bottom, and you pick out the essential details you are fishing for. This is about your eyes and nothing more. In fact, no one should ever notice what you're doing. Your eyes contact a subject matter first, and they determine the direction your analysis will take. Focus them properly, give them the right target, and process the data you get.

- **High comprehension levels.**

To be an effective speed reader, you need high levels of understanding. That always takes place in the mind, so you must be sober and mentally upright. You also need to have the right set of filters to ensure your biases aren't clouding your comprehension and analysis. Your processing speed has to be proportional to the visual speed you possess. You should be able to compile several traits and pick up clusters of information at one go so you can sort, analyze, and conclude swiftly. It isn't just about understanding your subject; it's also about understanding different traits and characters. If you're quick at establishing baselines for the people you interact with, this part will come naturally to you. Having a firm knowledge of a person's baseline makes it easier for you to analyze them accurately during critical situations when you must take fast action.

- **Keep the main thing the main thing.**

A key aspect of becoming a good speed reader is the ability to not get distracted. Our eyes can easily get drawn to things that are intriguing but not necessarily helpful. Think about that time you were at the club with the boys, and that lady in red walked in with a figure like Sophia Vergara, and your eyes just got stuck on her cleavage the whole time she walked past you. That's a perfect case of eyes wandering off to unnecessary points that won't make you a good speed reader or communicator. In that distracted state, you failed to notice anything of value that would have actually helped get her number. For one to come out with factual information, you need accuracy. To be accurate, you need to be disciplined with your eyes and focus on the key points that matter. If you desire a fruitful outcome, invest more of your mental abilities and skills in the facts that will help you genuinely analyze the individual you wish to know better. Don't allow yourself to get distracted like everyone else if you're on a speed reading mission.

Chapter 02: Verbal and Non-verbal language

So far, you've learned that we communicate in various ways, not just with our words. Most of our interpretations and analyses of others consist of data accumulated outside the spoken word, so it's imperative that you get skilled at understanding both aspects of communication. In the following pages, you will learn the difference between verbal and nonverbal and the varying types of non-verbal communication.

What is verbal communication?

Verbal communication is conveying a message through words. That can be in both written and spoken form. To be an effective communicator, not only do you need to get better at speaking and sharing your ideas concisely, but you also need to develop active listening skills. Effective speaking involves three main areas: the words you choose, how you say them, and how you reinforce them with other non-verbal communication. As you might have guessed, you cannot isolate the transmission of your message from non-verbal communication. In fact, there are many times when you could communicate with just non-verbal signals—for example, shrugging your shoulders to show you don't know something, or silently walking up to someone and giving them a hug to show your concern and affection for them—but it's almost impossible to communicate verbally without some form of non-verbal reinforcement.

Therefore, while it's important to consider your vocabulary, tone of voice, and pace, learning how your body communicates will be equally as important, if not more. It will also enable you to learn to read and analyze people better as they transmit their messages. In a later part of this book, we will talk about advanced techniques to help you develop your listening and speaking skills, but for now, let's dissect the weight that your tone carries when communicating with others.

How tone can communicate the unspoken thoughts

Do you know what your tone says about your personality, intentions, and emotions? Most people hardly give their tone a second thought. That's why it's so easy for a master communicator to read and analyze these people. The tone someone uses can help you figure out fairly quickly the direction of that conversation.

Suppose you're in a room with a stranger who introduces himself as a fan of your work. The words he speaks say he's friendly and admirable of what you do, but his tone hints at anger, jealously, and even resentment. Such a person unknowingly alerts you that you had best protect yourself and tread with caution. The tone and volume of our voice can reveal a lot about our brewing emotions. Sound frequencies create vibrations, so when reading people, notice how their tone of voice fluctuates throughout the interaction. Become aware of how that affects you. Ask yourself: Does this tone feel soothing? Or is it snippy, whiny, or abrasive?

When I was training myself to analyze people's voices better, I would often close my eyes (when appropriate) to focus on using my sense of hearing. I noticed that my ears would perk up as soon as my eyes were no longer in play, and that enabled me to have a deeper "feel" of the person and the emotions their voice was conveying. That isn't to say visual cues aren't necessary. Of course, we can tell a lot by looking at someone's face, and we will be discussing how to do that as well, but I think recent studies confirm how important the voice is. Think about your favorite radio presenters. Yes, I know most of us are stuck on Spotify and Apple Music, but if you've been around long enough to appreciate radio presenters, then you've had this experience already. These guys interact with us only through voice. That forces us to rely on analyzing and reading their personality solely through the sound frequencies they send us as they speak and present. Notice how your preferred presenter is only a favorite because they align with the desired personality trait that you've associated with him or her despite knowing little else but their voice and how they use it. When we talk about emotional intelligence, you'll realize how important it is to analyze and pick up signals from people through the various communication channels they use. And in our current world of Zoom and other technologies that make it possible for audio-only or virtual interactions, learning to detect emotions from tone of voice becomes a coveted superpower that all masterful communicators need. As I became more aware of voice and the subtle emotional information it conveys, I realized many emotions leak out during conversations. People have learned a lot about body language, and they've focused on controlling their body language, but very few people know about the emotions portrayed by their voice. Researchers now claim that voice can tell a lot about a person's character, education level, race, or ethnicity. With all this new research popping up, the main take-home message for you is to learn to pick up unspoken emotions and thoughts with practice and conscious attention to what someone is saying. Of course, that circles back to the importance of listening. You cannot read and analyze people well if you don't stop and fully listen to what people say. Accurately understand their intentions and get a feel for the unspoken emotions that leak out as they speak.

Understanding non-verbal communication

Non-verbal communication is the act of conveying a feeling, thought, or idea through some form of physical gesture, facial expression, or posture. Non-verbal communication plays a significant role in our lives. Your ability to establish meaningful, engaging interactions and to build instant trust is predicated on your body language as well as your aptitude for reading and accurately analyzing and responding to the signals others send you. The main form of non-verbal communication is body language. It takes various forms, and since there's no universal body language as different cultures have different forms of communication, it can be a vast and complex subject. However, we will stick to the American culture in our exploration and focus on sharing interpretations and meanings that apply mainly to this part of the world. After this book, my suggestion would be to continue your education and learn how other cultures interpret and convey their non-verbal cues.

Types of non-verbal communication

Remember the previous process we went through to describe how communication works? The same applies to non-verbal communication; you will need a packaged (encoded) message transmitted through a medium (e.g., face, body, etc.). The receiver will then decode and interpret the message. When it comes to the medium through which the non-verbal message is transmitted and how it is interpreted and analyzed, you'll need to familiarize yourself with the various types of nonverbal communication. These primarily involve the person's face, physical appearance or posture, eyes, and the space around his or her body.

Facial expressions
When was the last time you keenly observed someone's face and the various movements a person makes while speaking? You can deduce a lot from watching a person's facial expression. Is he smiling or frowning? Does his tone of voice align with the expression on his face?
If you start paying close attention to people's faces, you'll realize that some non-verbal actions are pretty ambiguous and open to interpretation. Depending on where you are in the world and who you're talking to, different expressions will mean different things. However, there are certain facial expressions that experts determine are globally accepted. Expressions of anger, fear, sadness, and happiness tend to be pretty consistent no matter where you are in the world.

Eye Gaze
When we talk about eye gaze, we're referring to blinking, a rolling of the eyes, staring, glaring, and so on. There's a way in which someone will look at you with admiration in their eyes. By contrast, another might look at you, and you'll freak out because of how creepy it is. In both cases, the eyes still conveyed pretty important information. In the American culture, a stable look in the eye is often associated with honesty. If someone looks you in the eye and he or she has steady eye movement, you're dealing with a good person. That's one of the reasons

people going for job interviews need to work on their nonverbal communication.

That's not to say that quick eye movements are all bad. There's a time and place for quick eye movements, such as when one is excited. So before analyzing someone's eye movement as bad, bring to bear the context and the personality of the person. We'll talk more about the different eye movements and their basic interpretations in a separate chapter.

Proxemics
I find this aspect of non-verbal communication quite intriguing. Did you know every human being needs a certain amount of space to feel comfortable around different people in their lives? Some need more space than others, and if we can observe more carefully the distance someone gives themselves, we can deduce a lot about their personality and intentions. Proxemics describes the generally accepted distance or space between people and what that could mean under certain circumstances. As a form of nonverbal communication, proxemics can be explained in two ways - interference as the actual communication or the distance maintained during verbal communication. Interference is when someone deliberately invades the space you feel belongs to you without your consent. That naturally triggers all kinds of interpretations, including confrontation, disrespect, recklessness, and carelessness on the part of the intrude. If, however, the person interfering is considered a very close friend, the interpretation might be less hostile and

antagonistic. It might even prove that the other person deeply cares about you.

When it comes to distance during a verbal conversation, you can deduce a lot, including how intimate the conversation is or how comfortable the person is around you. The amount of space between conversing individuals is highly influenced by the level of familiarity, social norms, personalities, cultural preferences, and expectations.

There are for zones to become aware of. The intimate zone is from 0-2 feet. The personal zone is between 2 -4 feet, social distance is between 4 - 12 feet, and public distance is anything over 12 feet. When strangers enter the wrong zone, discomfort is usually the natural outcome, and most people try to escape that situation as fast as possible.

As a general rule of thumb, you always want to start your business relationships in the social zone. Once you've established trust and connection, you can work your way up to the personal zone. I also encourage you to be more mindful of context whenever you're making a move into personal space because that distance will vary depending on the person's personality, cultural beliefs, and how affluent he or she is. I've noticed that more affluents persons demand more personal space. Surprisingly, even the more attractive women in our society seem to prefer more personal space when you're interacting with them.

Paralinguistics

We briefly touched on his earlier, so it's time to define and understand what paralinguistic means and why it's considered an essential aspect of non-verbal communication. Suppose you were sitting at the bar with your buddies and a lovely group of women walked by, and a few of them smiled in your direction. You immediately spot the one you'd like to talk to and ask your friends which of them would like to be your wingman for the night. Both of them say that they would be interested. However, the first responds slowly, dragging his voice in a low and insecure tone and volume. The other friend responds quickly and loudly, showing lots of enthusiasm in his voice. How would you interpret this response?

If it were me (and it has been a few times), I'd deduce that the second friend is more confident, enthusiastic, and more likely to be a great wingman. All that just from the speed and loudness of the respondent's voice? Yes, absolutely.

It's likely that the first guy was just saying yes to please me, or it could be that he might be interested yet feels too insecure and unsure about his chances of winning with these attractive ladies. That is what paralinguistics is all about. It describes the subtle cues that accompany the spoken word, separate from the actual words being spoken. Paralinguistics is more than just tone of voice; it's also the pitch and the volume used. When we talked about how the voice can leak out emotions, we touched on an aspect of paralinguistics. Think about it for a moment. Can you not detect when someone is joyful, angry, hesitant, fearful, or sad even if they don't flat out tell you?

Many times while growing up, your parents relied on paralinguistics when communicating with you. Sometimes you'd walk into the room, and your mom would immediately know something was wrong. She'd ask, "What's wrong?" and even if you said you were okay, she still pried until you finally caved and told her about the bully who took your lunch. Your mom was no magician; she just paid attention to your non-verbal communication.

Gestures
Gestures are signals or movements that we deliberately do as a way of communicating meaning. Gestures can work with or without words. I'm sure you've seen or used some hand gestures yourself (waved, pointed a finger, raised your hand, etc.). In today's technological world of texting and social media, gestures are commonplace, and I've seen text communications made up entirely of gestures only. Suppose you familiarize yourself with as many different gestures as possible. In that case, you could potentially stand at a distance and observe any two people communicating, and you'd have a pretty good read on the nature of their interaction. Emotions like anger, joy, and frustration are easy to read through gestures. Great communicators make it a point to align all their gestures with the intended words and emotions.

Appearance

Have you ever come across a person wearing gothic makeup and a T-shirt that says, "I hate everyone?" I have, and it didn't exactly make me feel like chatting them up. I've also been in that uncomfortable situation where a woman comes into the office wearing a casual Friday t-shirt with some feminist remark on her back. Like it or not, how we dress and present ourselves in the world speaks volumes about who we are. There are various ways to analyze and interpret who someone is, what they do, and where they are going in life just based on their appearance.

Dressing has a lot to do with someone's personality, beliefs, and perceptions. Aspects such as color and hairstyles also make a significant statement. For instance, people who like bright colors tend to be vibrant, outgoing, and sociable in their personalities. If you dig deeper into color psychology, experts of the subject matter will tell you that colors are often associated with feelings, moods, and behaviors. Interior designers rely on this principle when they decorate rooms for their clients. Before decorating, a good interior designer will strive to understand a particular room's intended emotions and moods. By understanding their client's driving emotion and motive, they are better equipped to create something appealing and exciting to the end consumer.

Not surprisingly, we also know that how others perceive an individual depends mainly on that person's appearance and how they carry themselves around people. A study conducted in 1996 concluded that appearance might even affect one's earning capacity. These conclusions came about as a result of investigating attorneys. The researchers involved realized that attorneys who were more attractive in appearance as compared to their colleagues were rated higher in their job and subsequently earned 15% more.

Lastly, we need to consider that culture will play a huge role in determining perceptions of appearance. For example, in many African countries, having a large body size is associated with being wealthy, healthy, and higher social status. But in most Western countries, the opposite is true. Larger size bodies are often considered unhealthy, and being slim is what everyone strives for. Before making your analysis of someone's appearance, keep these things in mind.

Haptics
Haptics involves touching to interact. Infants and young children rely heavily on this form of communication to bond with their caregivers. A study done by Harry Harlow suggested that when children are deprived of touch, their growth and development can be significantly impeded. But it's not just for children. Adults value touching as long as it's done in the right way at the right time. And when someone touches you, there are many meanings they could be trying to convey, from sympathy to longing and desire and everything in between.

What matters is to understand when and how to use touch so that it doesn't come across as creepy or intrusive. And even here, we need to be mindful of context and culture if we want touch to work in our favor. Touching someone the right way could immediately soothe them, establish a connection between the two of you, and cause the other person to feel loved depending on how you do it.

When someone touches you, it's necessary to learn how to identify the message being conveyed. Is it a friendly touch? Are they hiding ill intentions? We'll through various forms of touch in an upcoming chapter so you can become more aware of how others are using touch to send you messages.

Artifacts
Our modern civilization has become infatuated with artifacts, and each usually means something different than the person values. One of the trainers at my gym is a great example because he's got lots of body tattoos. I asked him once what some of them meant, and he eagerly gave me a story of how each one came to be. You might not always see tattoos on a body; sometimes, it is a cat picture on

social media profile or a bracelet won by the person. Usually, this is more than just a picture or an ornament. The image or jewelry typically reflects something about the individual's personality, identification, and beliefs. If you're observant enough, you can already deduce quite a bit about that person as they are communicating through these artifacts.

Uniforms are also an example of artifacts. A sailor or marine soldier walks into a coffee shop, and you immediately know what they do. In fact, would you ever recognize a police officer if they didn't wear a uniform on the streets and ride in that loud, conspicuous car? Wouldn't you feel a bit weird being treated by a doctor in the hospital who didn't wear the appropriate attire? Having these markers and artifacts is a socially acceptable way for us to communicate who we are, what we do, and at times, what we believe. Learn to pay more attention to the various ways people are telling more about them through their artifacts.

The power of non-verbal communication

In the 1960s, Dr. Mehrabian and colleagues conducted an experiment that exhibited how powerful non-verbal communication can be. In the study, the participants were given recordings of the word "maybe." These recordings reflected three things, namely favor, disfavor, and neutrality. Photos of females who were demonstrating the same three emotions were also shown to the participants. They were then asked to deduce the emotions that were associated with each photo and recording. The participants were better able to analyze and decipher the feelings of the females in the pictures. In another similar study by Dr. Mehrabian, participants could

pick meanings of words from the voice tone used (Smith,2020). In both studies, we can easily s the authenticity that comes with non-verbal communication. People might get away with "faking words," but non-verbal cues are very hard to fake.
What makes non-verbal communication so powerful is the ability to enhance authentic communication. That positively impacts all critical areas of life, whether you want to be a better communicator in your personal relationships or at work. There are three prominent roles non-verbal communication plays: conveying straightforward meaning, unleashing a hidden message, and emphasizing parts of your message.

Conveying straightforward meaning is about ensuring the correct message and meaning is sent. Sometimes there are no words to describe how you feel. For example, think about when the tragic accident of the basketball legend Kobe Bryant happened, and his wife received the news that both her husband and daughter had died in a helicopter crash. If you were a close family friend going to pay your condolences, it would be hard to find the right words to express your feelings toward her loss. In such moments, non-verbal communication such as a touch or hug and your eyes would convey much more and even offer soothing relief to the family than all the fancy words in the dictionary.

Another aspect of this is substitution which in the case of the tragedy mentioned above would mean you don't even try to say how sorry you are. You simply use body language such as a firm, reassuring hug, gestures, and eye contact to show the grieve-stricken family that you feel their anguish as well. Substitution is also what the deaf and hearing-impaired often rely on because they cannot use voice to convey a message.

When it comes to unleashing hidden meanings, nonverbal communication does it quite well because it's easy to hide emotions when writing a text to someone but almost impossible to "pretend" that you're not mad or sad while standing face to face with that same person. When attempting to read and analyze someone, I find it best to do it in person because it enables me to listen to their words and observe all their non-verbal cues. Half the time, someone might speak one thing, and their body language might send the opposite message.

Lastly, nonverbal communication is excellent when you wish to emphasize something important. If you'd like to know what someone considers important, notice the things they tend to animate more as they speak. By paying attention to the accent, one uses or the words most emphasized, you can pinpoint what one values.

How body language is communicating different moods

Let's consider how different personalities and gender differences affect how we communicate. It shouldn't be too hard to deduce that with some individuals, analyzing their emotions just by observing their body language will be easy to do. For example, think of a woman who is highly emotional and spontaneous in her expressions. Such a person is easy to read when angry, unhappy, excited, sad, etc. When such a woman is angry, she is likely to make spontaneous hand gestures, frown, or even use the silent treatment to express her emotions. Women tend to be associated with lower emotional control and spontaneity, which in some ways (though not always) makes it easy to read their mood just by analyzing their body language.

Most men, however, aren't considered very emotionally expressive or spontaneous. They are, in fact, known for their calm approach toward situations regardless of the context. That is, of course, an oversimplification and only applies to some instances. Imagine for a moment interacting with a cool-headed dude like Dominic Toretto from The Fast and the Furious. He would be difficult to read and analyze because his non-verbal communication is pretty dialed down. Conversely, Roman Pearce, also one of the main characters in the same movie franchise, is overly emotional, and his body language communicates his mood all the time. Observing and analyzing him would quickly tell whether he is happy, stressed, afraid, panicking, sad, or angry.

When it comes to reading moods, it comes down to the other person's personality and disposition and your ability to accurately analyze what they are attempting to convey.

Men and women differ in their non-verbal communication.

Many studies indicate that women fare better than men at recognizing and interpreting non-verbal cues. Some researchers also suggest that women are low power communicators meaning that a female is less likely to use a firm power hand when communicating (National Communication Association, 2011). According to the researchers, women exhibit low social power in their non-verbal communication, and that's quite the opposite of what their male counterparts do. Perhaps this has something to do with social conditioning and how men have always been viewed as a superior gender. Again, as with all generalizations, we need to acknowledge that this may not apply to all women. Think about a woman like Hilary Clinton and other powerful women in leadership positions. You might even consider powerful women throughout history, such as Cleopatra and Queen Elizabeth I. I am confident these women demonstrated high power of non-verbal communication.

Am I in control of my body language?

How aware are you of your non-verbal communication? Do you know whether you exhibit low or high power communication? There are some key things you want to take into account as you conduct a self-analysis.

- General appearance

Your general appearance is always going to be an essential aspect of your overall non-verbal communication. Women tend to go deeper than men fussing over the nitty-gritty of the things that make them look the way they want, e.g., makeup, trendy clothes, accessories, and so on. You might have noticed your girlfriend spend a fortune in getting her nails, eyelashes, and lips done so that she can establish a particular look. Not all women do this, of course, but I think each woman (to some degree) invests in her grooming and general appearance far more than the average man.

As men, we are less specific, so we probably have fewer fashion and grooming products options. Most men, however, do invest time and energy in their facial hair and their bodies. The beard is a standard accessory that many men work hard to nurture because it's associated with dominance. There's also a belief that beards increase head size in men, and who doesn't want to have a big head?

Regardless of your fashion taste, be more intentional about your dress code and grooming practices so that your general appearance can make the right kind of statement.

- Touch

We talked about the power of touch in communication. Are you aware of how you are using touch when communicating with others? People who are sensitive to the needs of others often include touch in their conversations. Women tend to use touch more than men in their non-verbal communication to convey care, affection, concern, and nurturance. For example, a female friend trying to comfort her colleague who just received terrible news is likely to rub the back of the unhappy one to assure them that everything will be fine. When men use touch, it is often to assert power or control over others. The pat on the back or touch on the shoulder is highly linked to power and dominance rather than care. How are you using touch to connect and communicate with others?

- Space

You want to become aware of how much space you need and how much space you give others when interacting. Are you one of those people who likes to keep a lot of distance between you and someone you're talking to? Or are you the opposite and enjoy being up close and personal even with people you don't have a personal relationship with? I've noticed that men tend to stand closer to women while having face-to-face interaction, but they maintain a little more distance when conversing with fellow men. Sometimes the drive to stand close to members of the opposite sex is driven by romantic desire. Other times it's a show of dominance and superiority depending on the man in question. Women generally prefer a little more distance when in conversation with a man, and they prefer a side-by-side stance when conversing with a man. With fellow females, they seem to be pretty comfortable being super close during face-to-face conversations. You should always be intentional with the space between you and the other person to avoid misunderstandings.

Standing too close might cause you to come across and creepy, and standing too far could make you appear cold and disinterested.

- Other cues

You should also observe how you use your hands, feet, eyes, and the most common facial expressions you make, especially in social situations. Ask a trusted friend to record you so you can rewatch how you carried yourself during a party or public gathering. You could also spend some time in front of a mirror and try smiling, frowning, etc., to see how your face changes with each new move. That might sound silly, but it usually offers excellent insight into what your body is doing when you're engaged with other people.

Body language changes depending on a person's intentions

Intention is everything when it comes to effective communication. You can make someone feel important, understood, or rejected just by packaging your non-verbal cues with the right intention. Whenever you identify the objective of the message you wish to convey, an intention is set. As long as you keep it simple and unambiguous, the receiver is likely to interpret the meaning of your message. The same holds true when you're analyzing people. The more straightforward the intent is, the easier it will be to decode their message even if you don't share that person's cultural, religious, or educational background.

Often we will enter into a conversation purely focused on our agenda. Whenever I do that, my body language is always different from when I enter into a discussion to understand and actively listen to others. The difference in body language between a person who intends to have their way and one who wants to listen and understand is like night and day. People can always sense this. My suggestion is to set your mind to hold the intention of being a strong listener whenever you're engaged in conversation. That's the right frame of mind for someone who wants to get good at reading people and developing instant rapport. A fantastic hack I can share with you here is to practice being detached from that final outcome. In other words, despite your desire to build rapport and instantly read someone, be okay with failing at it. Don't make that the primary goal. Instead, the primary goal should be to get the most out of that particular interaction. And that includes the other person as well. If everyone involved can come away feeling valued and understood, I consider that a successful exchange. Enter into each conversation in a way that honors the other person. It's not about becoming the next sherlock holmes here. It's about creating genuine and meaningful connections.

Chapter 03: Body Language

Certain gestures such as the "manual rhetoric" of Roman orators and the general carriage and deportment of the whole body have been studied since Classical times. In the fourth century BC in Greece, upper-class men cultivated an upright, firm stance and an unhurried gait, choosing instead to take long strides. This, they consciously conditioned themselves into doing so they could distinguish themselves as persons of leisure. That way, people wouldn't mistake them for artisans or slaves who always had to hurry to get work done. It also distinguished them from women who moved in a mincing manner taking tiny steps. And speaking of women, courtesans seemed to have their own mannerisms as they moved about. They would sway their hips from side to side while walking more pronouncedly, making it easier to identify them from the rest of the women. To assume that body language and the study of it is new is folly. It's a subject matter that has been deeply integrated into our psyche as humans, and we'll be analyzing people through body language for centuries.

In classical Rome, strictly moderated and limited gestures were regarded as an indication of a temperate and self-controlled character. This quality was a requirement for anyone who desired to become a Roman aristocrat and orator.

During the Renaissance era in Europe, writings on body language were quite prevalent. Seventeenth-century physiognomists like Giovanni Della Porta and Charles Lebrun codified the facial expressions of emotion and character. Their investigations and those of their contemporaries Giovanni Bonifacio and John Bulwer were conducted on the assumption that there existed a universal natural language of expression and gesture that could be understood by all people anywhere in the world.

In the nineteenth century, the works of Charles Darwin on animal and human emotions tended to support the view that physical expressions might be biologically inherited. In turn, the physical conditions under which people live and the bodily deportment and habitual actions they perform have consequences for the structures of their bodies. We know this to be accurate thanks to the discoveries made by paleoarcheologists, who have used the evidence of excavated skeletons to offer generalizations about the body habits of the past. There are also a few modern ethnologists and zoologists like Desmond Morris who stress the similarities between bodily movements used by humans and those observed in animals to express hostility, fear, dominance, or territoriality.

Why is Body language so important in our lives?

What if I told you there was a simple way through which you could get almost anything you desire? You could secretly know what someone is thinking. You could ensure that your next date never forgets you and instead desires you even more. Imagine finally getting that raise without the need to work harder than you're already doing. Body language is the key to all of this and more. Evidence backs up this claim, and we find that people who are excellent at analyzing people tend to excel in their careers, have better relationships, and get away with a lot more than those with poor people skills. If you're thinking there's magic or sorcery behind excellent people reading skills, let me put you at ease. Body language is a skill anyone can learn. Those that take the time to develop this skill find that life changes for the better. You need to remember that all our interactions, projects, and desires rely on human relationships in one form or another at the end of the day. To get the kind of life you've always dreamed of, you'll need to master the skill of dealing with people. The more you can read, analyze and influence people in a positive way, the easier it will be to have your way, and that's why body language is a critical life skill for any ambitious person.

The science of body language

In the late 1960s, psychologist Albert Mehrabian conducted a study leading to a communication model that many use today. Although most of it is often misquoted and misinterpreted, the main idea remains true because we communicate with more than just words. Mehrabian's study specifically focused on communication where feelings and attitudes were the key factors. He often says that his findings — 93% of our communication is non-verbal communication and only 7% is through words— shouldn't be assumed as accurate across the board.

By looking at how people communicate, you probably might get an accurate read of what they are attempting to pass on. But non-verbal communication is much more than noticing a person's face forming a frown or looking at their hand gestures and eye movement. There are some neural connections and interactions that are involved. Going back to the start of this book, where I said the brain is involved in non-verbal communication, you should know that non-verbal communication is innate. In fact, there's growing evidence that the brain's right hemisphere controls non-verbal communication. As you might know, we each have a right and left hemisphere in our brains. The left governs our verbal communication, and the right regulates non-verbal communication. One evidence supporting this fact is seen in individuals who suffered some form of trauma on their right hemisphere of the brain. Often these individuals are incapable of recognizing and interpreting facial expressions. These people could still process verbal communication, but they couldn't read or analyze them non verbally.

In the right hemisphere, the limbic system seems to be responsible for regulating your body language. The limbic system is made up of various parts, including the amygdala, hippocampus, and insula. You don't need to concern yourself with the details of each aspect of your brain. Just know that the limbic brain is the one receiving information about your emotions and triggers the body to respond to them accordingly. When there's a perceived or real physical or psychological threat, the amygdala is activated, and in turn, your body reacts. Why does this matter when understanding non-verbal communication?

Given our new understanding that the limbic system controls emotions and regulates body language, you should realize how this affects non-verbal communication in yourself and others. All the decisions we make in both personal and professional situations are influenced by emotions. Most of the time, logical processes are only rational justifications that are based on emotional decisions. If everything we do is associated with some form of emotion and non-verbal communication is influenced by emotions regulated by the limbic system, then non-verbal communication may be controlled by what happens in the limbic brain. The more you can control your feelings, the easier it becomes to control your body signals. And the more attuned you become with reading emotions, the easier it becomes to analyze what's really going on with another.

The East and The West Differ

Across different cultures (even within the U.S), you might find a variety of meanings in the little gestures people portray in different scenarios. Move further into the world to Eastern or African cultures, and body language becomes significantly different. Signals we consider positive might be negative in certain parts of the world. Although it wouldn't be too hard to decipher the meanings of the most common body language signals, even in a completely foreign country, it's essential to understand the most common or globally practiced body movements so you can interpret them accurately. Let's talk about the most obvious - eye contact. In western-based countries, direct eye contact is encouraged and seen as assertiveness and confidence. A bold glance shows you believe in yourself. It's a sign of personal responsibility and high self-esteem (at times even honesty). In some eastern-based countries and many parts of Africa, some glances beyond the typical brief moments are considered a sign of aggression or confrontation. Depending on your gender, direct eye contact is discouraged tremendously.

In fact, respect and grace are associated with a lack of direct eye contact, especially between members of the opposite sex. Touch is also a sensitive body language depending on your gender and where you are. Most middle eastern countries prefer little to no contact. There are very few occasions where handshakes are exchanged, and physical contact with strangers or people you're unfamiliar with is usually discouraged. By contrast, you'll find some Arabic countries that value the body language of touch greatly. Even men kiss each other and hold hands for lengthy periods as an indication of trust and friendship. Latin cultures also rely a lot on touch. The culture encourages men and women to engage in plenty of physical contact (kissing and touching) to signify friendship and trust. This would be seen as highly inappropriate and perhaps even viewed as immoral in other western cultures. We'll discuss the impact of culture in a little while, but the take-home point is simply this. Be mindful of your environment and the cultural background of the persons you're analyzing to make the correct interpretations.

Chapter 04: Body Language Cues And Meanings

Are you aware that there are over 20 muscles in the face that constitutes over 10,000 facial expressions? Now that you're more aware of how your body moves when interacting with others, it's time to shift focus are learn to decode the different meanings behind body cues. This is literally the kickoff point in your ability to confidently read, analyze and interpret others through their body language.

The way we move, walk, sit and stand can give a skilled individual a deep understanding of who we are. Each of us expresses our body language in one of four ways: light and bouncy movement, a soft and fluid movement, a dynamic and determined movement, or a precise and bold movement. Each of these movements has different meanings and coincides with one of the four energy types. Let's analyze each a little more closely through the lens of this profiling system.

Light, bouncy, and animated movement is Type 01 Energy.
It is important to remember that this energy type profiling is mainly drawn from facial features and body language. So type one is exhibited as a buoyant walk as though one has a spring in their step. This energy type will stand and sit with a lot of

movement, shifting positions often. As you observer such an individual, you'll notice they appear restless and fidgety. Perhaps they don't like to sit or stand or focus on any one thing for very long. They often sit with legs crisscrossed or very comfortably on the floor. If you've come across people who seem overly hyper, constantly bumping into things and people, then you've experienced this type of energy profiling.

Soft, fluid and flowing is Type 02 Energy.
Type two is smooth and graceful in their walk. They take longer steps and keep their feet close to the ground, and there's no bounce in their step. Instead, you observe a very fluid and flowing movement. When the person sits or stands, they tend to form an invisible S curve or make a relaxed bend holding their head to the side.

Active, reactive, substantial, and dynamic is Type 03 Energy.
What you'll notice first is a particular determination in this person's step. Their feet are firmly planted on the ground, and they take quick and brisk steps. Everyone can hear them coming. You can even hear them sit because all their movement is very deliberate. Observe such a person sitting or standing, and you'll notice all kinds of formed angles either with their legs crossed, one leg pulled up resting on top of the other, hands-on waist, and so many other variations.

Bold, constant, still, and precise is Type 04 Energy. This type of energy walks very upright and maintains a still stately manner with slight movements in their limbs and body. When they sit, they are very upright and like to keep a straight posture almost all the time. Both feet are always on the ground, and they like to fold their hands or hang them gently on the side. We might call this a more formal look because the person is just naturally erect, poised, and very structured in their movement. Many calm men possess this energy profile because they maintain a very posed and consistent pace as they walk or speak. If walking, the man will typically have a constant rate and doesn't speed up or slow down even if he is late. In fact, this energy profile only cares about being the authority of his own movement and singing to his own tune.

 Now, you might notice that you likely exhibit a mix of these even with your own movement, and that's okay. We all have more than one profile, but you'll realize that one of them is predominant to you. The same will be true for the people you're analyzing. Observe them long enough, and you'll know which is their dominant energy type.

Body cues and what they signal

We will look at two broad categories when discussing signals and meaning: positive or open body language and negative or closed body language. By reading these cues, you'll figure out how receptive others are to you or the situation. At any given time, a person is either open or closed from their external environment. Whether it's at a BBQ party, a networking event, family gathering, board room meeting, giving a presentation, or dining with you on that first date, people will always show you what state they are in through their non-verbal communication.

Open body language examples

• Open palms:
Open palms are a hand gesture that demonstrates openness. Instead of hiding them in their pockets, behind their backs, or holding a closed fist, the person will display their hands. It is usually a sign that the person is being honest and sincere with you.

Evolutionarily, when we see closed palms, our brains receive the signal that we might be in danger (the hidden hands could be carrying a weapon of hiding something life-threatening). Our limbic brain automatically communicates to the rest of the brain, and we become reactive. But sometimes, the other person is simply unaware of their non-verbal communication. So it's not always a good idea to immediately get defensive when you don't see someone's hands. However, it's always a good sign when the person you're talking to is aware enough to show you their open hands.

How you can use it:
When engaged with others in conversation, ensure your hands are open most of the time and that people

can see them. It's also best to keep the palms facing upward as much as possible.

• The eyebrow flash:
When someone does an eyebrow flash, you'll see their eyebrows raise slightly for a fraction of a second. This is usually a sign of interest. People tend to use this to show professional interest, either to give approval or agree to something. It can also be used to seek confirmation or even thank someone.

Think of it as a quick nonverbal "yes." In a romantic setting, the eyebrow flash indicates romantic interest. It can also be used in a social setting between two friends when they recognize each other. It signals to the other person delight in the encounter. Whenever we use the eyebrow flash, we call attention to the face. Teachers and speakers often use it as a way of saying "Listen to this!" or "Look at me!" depending on context.

Not all cultures see this as a positive cue, however. For example, the Japanese find this cue indecent, so I would avoid it entirely when engaging with Japanese people.

How you can use it:
Use the eyebrow flash when you see someone you like or who you want to like you. Give them a quick eyebrow flash followed by a warm smile. If you're going to get the attention of someone or have them pay closer attention to what you're about to say, raise your eyebrows right before you deliver the message.

And if you're on the receiving end of a conversation and want to show your interlocutor that you're interested, raise your eyebrows!

• The equal handshake:
Have you ever had a really awkward and yucky handshake? Or maybe one that was just downright weak and clumsy? Handshakes are really important when building mutual rapport, and they can tell us a lot about the other person. A handshake can tell us whether the person is nervous, submissive, aggressive, domineering, or confident.

When you shake hands, you want to make sure it's not too firm and dominant, but at the same time, it shouldn't come across as weak. That's why learning an equal handshake is encouraged. There are several elements to a good handshake. Namely, maintaining good eye contact, having a warm, genuine smile, extending your arm with a slight bend at the elbow, keeping your fingers pointed downward while approaching the other person's hand, and most importantly, applying equal pressure during the handclasp. It's also best to lean forward toward the other person and make sure to do a slow release of the handshake after about two seconds. This type of handshake signals mutual respect, openness, confidence, and power. Yet, it leaves the other person feeling warm and fuzzy inside. Whenever you shake someone's hand, and they leave you with that special and good feeling, you can be sure they used this equal handshake technique on you.

How you can use it:
A good rule of thumb is to only shake hands when you know the other person is receptive and open to it. Always think about context and culture before extending a handshake to someone. If they are from Japanese culture, they might prefer a different form of greeting (such as bowing your head). If they are Italian, perhaps a kiss on the cheek is more welcome. If you're unsure how well a handshake will be received, consider a head nod or wait for another person to initiate it.

Always remember the part about applying equal pressure and be mindful of the age group you're interacting with. Older people require less pressure. People of a higher status in society like to determine the length and pressure of the handshake first, so go with that flow and be sure to reciprocate with an equal exchange for maximum bonding.

• Mutual gazing

This is another open body signal that shows interest. More prolonged eye contact, especially from people who are of high status, makes us feel favored. That is especially the case when receiving eye contact from celebrities and movie stars. Increased eye contact also indicated the other person might be curious. Please don't confuse with prolonged and direct eye contact, as most people associate that with aggression. Instead, make eye contact when you agree, when you're actively listening and nodding, and when you're exchanging ideas.

Research indicates that making eye contact just 30% of the time significantly increases the likelihood that your interlocutor will remember what you said. Interestingly enough, certain personality types naturally make eye contact while others struggle with this. If you're the type that struggles, start slowly and perhaps make your focal point areas like the forehead or in-between the eyes so the other person can still feel like you're mutually gazing at each other.

How you can use it:
Do a bit more eye gazing when you wish to bond with someone. Don't make it too direct and unnatural, as you might come across the wrong way. Make sure to glance away occasionally and only look them in the eyes with a soft face when the context of the conversation permits it.

- The head tilt

The head tilt is when a person tilts to one side, exposing their neck. This indicates openness because the neck is one of the most vulnerable areas in a person's body. The skin on the neck is much thinner and requires more protection, so when someone exposes their neck and throat, they are essentially opening up. They are showing you that they are comfortable enough around you to be vulnerable.

You'll often see a head tilt from women, especially if they are attracted to you. Still, it can also be used to indicate platonic interest. When a man does it, they usually indicate curiosity about what you're saying, especially if the head tilt is combined with a head nod. Studies of paintings in the last two millennia show that women are depicted three times often as men using the head tilt. Even in modern advertisements, we tend to see a woman tilting her head more often than we see men.

How you can use it:
See it more as a disarming behavior and use it whenever you want to ease a tense situation or get someone to open up. But don't use it too much, especially in official meetings or during sales pitches when the last thing you want is to come off "soft" and exposed.

Closed body language examples

• Crossed arms
Crossed arms are one of the most common cues for closed body language that you'll encounter. Practically everyone crosses their arms at some point or another. Most people do this are a protective or coping mechanism. They are likely to cross their arms when projecting anger, anxiety, stress, or even trying to soothe themselves from these emotions. Crossed arms are often done in public. I challenge you to observe yourself to see if you ever cross your arms while alone in the comfort of your home.

Sometimes you might notice someone will clench their fist and combine that with the crossing of the arms, tightening of the lips, or clenching their teeth. Research of over 1500 volunteers was conducted to find out exactly how the crossed-arms gesture made people feel. The volunteers were divided into two groups while attending a series of lectures. The first group was asked to keep their legs uncrossed, arms folded, and to take a relaxed sitting position. The second group did the same, except they were asked to cross their arms throughout the lectures. The outcome was that the second group learned and retained 38% less information than the group with unfolded arms. They were also more critical in their opinions about the lecturers and the lectures.

Of course, you need to be aware of other cluster cues to help you determine whether one is feeling cold or simply closing you off. And if you'd like to know how to handle someone with crossed arms, keep reading because later in the book, we'll talk about different ways to handle difficult people and their personalities.

• Crossed legs
This is when the feet are crossed, and one ankle lies on top of the other. It can be done while sitting, standing, or with feet on the table/stool. A person crossing their ankles typically indicates that they are uncomfortable and closed off. The tighter their ankles are locked in, the anxiety or stress the person might be experiencing. But there are some exceptions to this rule. For example, women wearing dresses or skirts tend to sit with their ankles locked which is generally not associated with a closed body language. However, if done for a prolonged period, it might be negative non-verbal communication.

Another exception to this is when you see ankles crossed while legs are outstretched on the floor. This can be a relaxed posture with the legs taking up space.

An extreme example of crossed legs is when a person locks their feet around the legs of a chair. That usually occurs under high-stress situations. I call this the "ejection seat" position because you'd only expect one to have such a position if they were about to be launched out of their seat.

• Neck rubbing
When people rub their necks, they usually mask their feelings of insecurity or mounting stress. For others, it's a stress-relieving mechanism. According to scientific studies, when the vagus nerve (the nerve on the side of the neck) is massaged, acetylcholine, a neurotransmitter that sends signals to the heart, causes the heart rate to go down. In more extreme cases, you might see the suprasternal notch (the part where your neck meets your clavicle) being touched. According to various studies, those who habitually rub the neck tend to be more pessimistic or critical than others.

• Fidgeting with objects
Fidgeting involves playing with nearby objects such as keys, coins, a pen, a ring, or a necklace. Sometimes people will use their fingers or hair to fidget too. It typically indicated boredom. Perhaps the person is bored of the conversation, the environment, or you (ouch!). When a person fidgets,

they are subconsciously longing for some sensory reassurance or exhibiting their anxiety. It could also be that they feel like they are running out of time or experiencing some kind of disappointment. Observations done at airports and railways stations found that people fidget a lot when traveling.

Interestingly, fidgeting is more pronounced when flying than traveling by train. This is exhibited through behavior such as checking tickets, taking out passports and putting them away, rearranging the hand baggage, dropping things and picking them up, and continually checking to make sure their wallet is in place. Could it be that flying brings more anxiety than train travel?

How you can use it:
If you are the one bored of a conversation, situation, or person, just start jangling your keys or coins in your pocket or hands. It could potentially come off as rude, but if you're certain you wish to terminate that encounter, this is a surefire way to get it done.

While there are many more examples of both open and closed body language signals across the board, let's move on to discuss hand gestures, and body proxemics.

Hand gestures

A hand gesture is part of body language communication. One moves their hands to accentuate or communicate an idea. Gestures influence the meaning we derive from a given message. When a person makes distinct hand gestures, they tend to come across as more confident.

If you're making hand gestures, I recommend keeping your hands between the top of your chest to the bottom of your waist. Moving your hands too high or too low can be distracting to your interlocutor. Now let's look at some common hand gestures and what data they can give you to analyze someone.

• Thumbs up: In many parts of the world, the thumbs-up is generally recognized as a sign of agreement. But if you are visiting Bangladesh, please avoid using this at all costs as it is considered an extreme insult.

• Thumbs down: Thumbs down is generally accepted as a "bad" or "no good" gesture. But did you know that during Roman times, this gesture was used to spell out death? Thank goodness there were no emojis at that time. Imagine how much trouble you'd be in if a Roman soldier sent you an emoji thumbs-down! As a general rule, even today (though we are no longer in the era of the Gladiator), someone sending you a thumbs-down gesture probably doesn't agree with your words, actions, or mannerisms. It can be viewed as a bit childish for someone to physically use this. Still, if you're having a virtual meeting or exchanging a chat, it's pretty standard for adults to use this gesture. It just means you need to establish a more positive rapport because your interlocutor is not amused by the current conversation.

• Handshake: We mentioned the importance of a good handshake, especially in the United States. This gesture is considered a form of greeting in many parts of the world. When done right, it signals to the other person that you are open, welcoming, and confident and that you respect and value their presence. However, not all cultures see handshakes in a positive light. In Russia, handshakes are not valued or seen in a positive light, so I would avoid extending handshakes if you ever visit Russian territory.

• "Listen Up!": This is a very strong gesture, and when someone uses it, they intend to draw your attention because they have something important to say.

• "Come Here" hand movement: In the United States, we use this hand gesture when we want to ask a person to come forward or do something for us. There are a variety of "come here" signals, most of which are considered negative so I advise using them with great precaution. There's the "forefinger beckon," which is more flirtatious (and sometimes creepy). You might see single people using it at nightclubs when they get hammered, and most decent girls always get offended. There's also the "full-arm" beckon (come here son), the "double-arm" beckon (come to me), the "side-arm" beckon (come on in), the "finger wave" beckon, and the provoker.

Again, in certain parts of the world like Asia, this gesture isn't acceptable. In the Philippines, for example, you could get arrested because it's incredibly offensive. In Singapore, it refers to "death," so pay attention to the environment when using it. So depending on where you are in the world, the beckon can be different and have totally different meanings.

• Clenched hand: A person with a solid fist
A person with a clenched fist-shaking it at you or punching it in the air is conveying intensity. It could be that they are making a very important point or acknowledging that they've just done something epic (you might see athletes doing this after they've scored). If, however, it is accompanied by an irritated voice and other negative cluster cues, you might be looking at someone who is feeling angry.

• I am magnanimous: If you're interacting with a person and they stretch out both hands palms facing toward you, we call that a godlike pose because it signals grandiosity.

• Growth: A person moving their hand or gesturing upward indicated some king of growth or increase. Typically this indicated expected growth, excitement, or direction where something is headed.

- This and that: Someone trying to convey two different ideas or contrast things can use their hands symbolically to represent them. It helps put distance between two things. You might notice the person will have open palms, separate their hands and raise each side as they talk about the two things or ideas for emphasis.

- Come together: A person brings both hands together as a way of showing two forces coming together as one. This tells you a lot about the person's intentions and the outcome they most want in that given situation.

- Stop: When someone flashes their palm at you, they want you to pause or stop. Perhaps you were in the middle of an explanation or asking a question. This should, however, be an exception and something that one uses rarely. If you notice the person uses this in their communication, understand you're dealing with a more aggressive and less empathetic personality.

- The V sign: The V sign with 2 fingers can mean the number 2, victory, what's up, or peace, depending on the angle and context. If the person has their palm facing toward themselves while holding up the two, they are essentially insulting you. It could be unintentional (like when British Prime Minister Margaret Thatcher did it to the public). Nonetheless, it's still a "screw you" type of message.

- Hand holding arm: This gesture is when a person places one touches their arm either to massage, scratch, or simply rest it on the other arm. Anytime this happens, the person might be signaling insecurity, doubt, anxiety, stress, or uncertainty. When it's a massage, this is often a self-pacifying exercise similar to a self hug. You'll need to combine this observation with other gestures to get the full scope of what's going on with the person.

- Prayer hands position: This is a humbling gesture and could signal a lot of things. For instance, if the person is Japanese, they might be saying "thank you" to you, or if they also a slight bow, it could be a form of greeting (many Asian cultures incorporate some form of this gesture as an honorable greeting technique). In India, it is common to see individuals holding this position and articulating "Namaste." For other religions, especially Christianity, the gesture is used to ask forgiveness and make themselves humble in your presence.

Body movements

How we hold our bodies can relay critical data for a keen observer. For instance, now that you know about open and closed body language, realize that when you see someone sitting with a closed posture, they could be hostile, unfriendly, and anxious. By contrast, someone with an open posture may indicate that they are open, friendly, and willing to interact with you. Posture can tell us a lot about a person's

personality, how confident they are and whether or not they want to engage in conversation with us.
If your interlocutor is sitting up straight, they convey that they are focused and present to what's going on. Sitting with the body hunched forward could imply that the person is indifferent, bored, or distracted by something. While reading body language, try to notice some of the signals the person is sending.

Open posture:
With an open posture, the person will keep the trunk of the body open and exposed.

Closed posture:
When it's a closed posture, the person will hide the body's trunk and keep their arms and legs crossed.

We should also talk about some of the things you can infer from the way an individual stands. For instance, leaning back on a wall or other support can suggest boredom or disinterest, especially if combined with a cluster of other behaviors like fidgeting and frowning. Leaning in toward you typically indicates interest and excitement, or curiosity. People who stand straight sometimes with their hands on their hips tend to be more confident, eager and could even be suggesting excitement. The most common standing posture is straight, with hands resting on the sides of the body. It usually indicates a willingness to engage and listen.

If, however, you're sitting with someone and they rest their head on their hands, depending on the context, they could be feeling bored, tired, or even strong interest in what you're saying. I cannot emphasize enough the importance of gathering a cluster of data before making a judgment.

Decoding the mouth:

Although you might think smiling is always a good thing, different smiles mean different things. The way a person smiles and how they position the lips tells you a lot.

With a truly genuine smile, the corners of the mouth turn upward, and the eyes narrow and wrinkle at the corners. Insincere smiles generally won't involve the eyes. Most of the time, a person will smile insincerely when they are hiding discomfort. You might also notice a partial smile or a smirk which often accompanies displeasure or contempt. This usually suggests disdain, dislike, or uncertainty. If the person you're talking to smiles and combines that with lasting eye contact, a long glance, or a head tilt, that could be an indication of attraction or romantic interest.

When it comes to the lips, compressed or narrowed lips could be indicative of unease. Quivering lips tend to suggest emotions of fear or sadness. Pursed lips are often signaling disagreement or brewing anger. When a person has open, slightly parted lips, it generally means they feel at ease and very relaxed around you.

What the eyes can tell you:

The eyes are often called the windows of the soul. By observing someone's eyes, you can deduce their mood, level of interest, and the hidden emotions they don't want you to know.

Blinking: If a person blinks rapidly, they are usually under some form of stress. Most people assume rapid blinking suggests dishonesty, but that isn't factual. Sometimes people blink when they're uncomfortable, afraid, worried about something, or working through a difficult problem.

Pupil dilation: Pupils dilate when we feel positively toward something or someone. Dilation happens in response to the arousal of the nervous system. Sometimes you'll see someone's pupil dilating either because there's a romantic attraction taking place or because they are infuriated or greatly afraid. If a person is bored and displeased, the pupils usually contract and get smaller.

Gaze direction: If you're trying to have a read of what someone is really interested in, just track the movement of their gaze. Our eyes can't help but wonder and follow what most interests us in any given situation. So if you're sitting across someone and you notice their gaze keeps moving in the direction of the buffet table, perhaps it's a good idea to save the talk until after they've eaten because nothing you say will be of greater value than their desire to eat at that moment. If you're having dinner with a woman and she keeps staring at the door or outside, then it's likely she would rather leave as soon as possible. You need to figure out whether it's you she doesn't want to be around or the restaurant.

People also move their eyes around when recalling information or memories while working through a problem or thinking about something difficult. Interestingly, the eyes tend to move downward or to one particular side depending on a person's personality and baseline. Yet another important reason to identify baselines first and foremost.

Engage in conversation with someone who keeps covering their eyes with their hands, rubbing their eyes, squinting, or closing their eyes briefly (long unnatural blinks). It could be that the person is feeling distressed or irritated, but they don't want to tell you. Some people block their eyes when faced with something they don't particularly want to deal with. Still, it could also be a show of disagreement or reluctance. For instance, your colleague knows it's their turn to work overtime on the weekend, but they want to clock out before you. When you call them out, instead of arguing, they unconsciously raise their hands to their eyes and then quietly and stressfully drag their feet back to their desk.

Breathing Clues

Did you know you can tell a lot about a person's emotional state and stress levels just by tracking their breathing? Whenever we get stressed, our breathing tends to increase rapidly, and it also becomes more shallow. Sometimes it's due to positive stress that leads to a sense of excitedness and thrill, or it might be due to negative stress, which stirs up worry, anxiety, and nervousness. Someone who takes long, deep breathes typically suggests calmness of thoughtfulness. You might come across individuals who are aware of non-verbal communication techniques. They might attempt to hide their emotional state by controlling their breath to suppress strong emotions like anger and jealousy. They might not be easy to pick up, but these emotions will start leaking out unconsciously if you hang around them long enough.

Arms:

People usually cross their arms when feeling vulnerable, anxious, or uninterested in considering another's perspective. However, this isn't the only meaning you can derive from crossed arms. Some people do it as a show of confidence. For example, suppose you're engaged in a conversation with someone impressive. They say something rather dramatic and immediately cross their arms while smiling as they lean back into the seat for maximum effect. That kind of move is used to exhibit confidence and control of the situation rather than vulnerability. In other cases, the arms offer a sense of protection or soothing sensation to the individual. In such cases, you're likely to observe the person holding something against the chest or putting an arm out to create distance. The person might use one arm to hold the other behind the back. It usually infers that the person isn't comfortable in that situation and needs to somehow hold themselves steady or protect themselves.

Legs and feet:

If you notice the person constantly taps their feet, jiggles their legs, or keeps shifting from foot to foot, they exhibit nervousness and restlessness. Crossed legs also suggest an unwillingness to hear what someone says, especially if this is combined with crossed arms.

When observing feet, the thing to note is the direction the feet face as the person interacts with you. If their feet point away, they may feel more like leaving the conversation than continuing it. If, however, their feet point toward you, that person indicates that they are engrossed in and thoroughly enjoying your conversation.

This chapter is far from exhaustive because there are many forms of body cues with various meanings. While it can be challenging to understand the slight shifts in each circumstance and the changes in facial expressions that tend to happen naturally throughout a conversation or social interaction, you'll better predict human behavior through practice and observation. The best way to understand body language and read people fast is to engage them in conversation and let them do most of the talking. Listen attentively, aim for some level of eye contact, and don't get too caught up in analyzing the person that you forget to listen to their words.

Context and Culture

Context refers to the circumstances surrounding the ongoing non-verbal communication. It's imperative to read body language through the lens of the present context. For example, crossing one's arms could mean a variety of things. Before making any deductions, consider the type of conversation you are having and the environment, timing, and any other external factors that might influence that particular action.

How culture influences non-verbal communication

We know how culture shapes our worldview, beliefs, and perceptions. It would be foolish to assume that it has no bearing on non-verbal communication and how we interpret what someone does. What might seem right in one culture might be considered highly insulting in another. Investing a little time to understand the basics of different cultures (especially the ones you're more likely to interact with) could mean the difference between success and failure in your relationship-building efforts. It could also hinder or accelerate your ability to accurately analyze the people in your life. Our world has become a global village where everything is interconnected by technology. Learning to read and understand people who don't live in your neighborhood or country is pretty handy when everything, even our careers, has become more digitalized.

Let's take the example of the different cultural rules when it comes to eye contact. In conversations, American custom demands eye contact between speaker and listener. Without it, people engaged in that conversation would be suspicious of each other. There's a common saying in the American culture that goes, "Don't trust anyone who doesn't look you in the eye," and many other western cultures seem to agree. By contrast, you can find several countries like Ghana, the Philippines, and many Hispanic countries that believe direct contact from a child to an adult is an act of disrespect. In the Middle East culture, direct eye contact from a woman to a man is an aggressive signal of sexual interest, and it's heavily shunned.

In Bangladesh, though direct eye contact is valued in conversations with peers, everyone —even adults— must show respect for an older person or people of higher status by keeping their eyes to the ground and speaking only when spoken to. In Japan, speakers are supposed to look at the listeners' neck or elsewhere, not into their eyes. (Oguibe, 1992)

Winking, a common non-verbal gesture in America that could mean a variety of things such as: "We are having fun, aren't we?", "That person over there is ridiculous, don't you think?", "Let that be our little secret," "I like you," or "I want to get sexually close to you." It all depends on the context. However, the same signal in Paraguay, Australia, and Nepal is considered vulgar, especially if done to the opposite sex. People would think you utterly rude in Hong Kong, Tunisia, and Bangladesh if you winked at them. In Nigeria, a wink at a child tells them they should leave the room immediately.

Hand gestures also vary depending on the culture. In the American culture, the "Okay" sign means strong approval or goodness. Still, to the French, the same gesture means "worthless" or "zero." If you want to show approval in France, you should do a thumbs up. If you're in Kenya, you should opt for a two thumbs up if you want to show approval, and if you're in Greece or the Middle East, you should avoid this gesture at all cost as it might be interpreted as "up yours!"

In Italy, a better gesture for happiness or praise is the "cheek screw," whereby you take your index finger, poke your cheek and twist it. You can also kiss your fingertips as a sign of happiness, joy, and utter approval of something or someone. The English and French people tend to keep their palms upward. In contrast, Italians keep their palms facing downward in most of the hand gestures and body movements.

If you're wondering how much physical contact or "touch" you can have with various cultures, a high-level overview will suffice. We consider Nothern Europe and the Far East to be non-contact cultures.

People generally stand as far away from each other as possible and have minimal physical contact with people they don't know well. Even accidentally brushing someone's arm on the street warrants an apology in such locations. By contrast, Southern Europe, Latin America, and some parts of the Middle East are considered high-contact cultures because physical touch is a big part of socializing. The rules are pretty complex and may differ depending on age, gender, ethnicity, profession, and status of the people involved. Be mindful and when you're uncertain, take a step back and observe how others are behaving before imposing your culture.

Section Two: Psychology and Personality Types

Chapter 05: What Is Psychology And Why Does It Matter?

The topic of psychology is broad and takes an entire lifetime to fully grasp (if you're lucky), but we don't have that much time here, so we'll take a crash course. We only need to learn enough about psychology and how to leverage this knowledge to read people. There's a lot of confusion over what psychology is, so let's start by looking at a couple of definitions.

According to The British Psychological Society, Psychology is the scientific study of people, the mind, and behavior. It's both a thriving academic discipline and a vital professional practice. That should help you see why psychology plays a role in the science of effective communication and people analysis.

American Psychology Association says it's the scientific study of the behavior of individuals and their mental processes. Psychology is a multifaceted discipline. It includes many sub-fields of study such as human development, sports, health, clinical, social behavior, and cognitive processes. I know both these definitions don't eliminate the ambiguity associated with this term but let's remind ourselves of how new this science is. Most of the advances in this scientific field happened over the past 150 years or so. But the origins can be traced back to ancient Greece, 400-500 years BC. The thing is, though, back then, it was integrated into philosophy. That's why great thinkers such as Socrates (470 BC - 399 BC), Plato (428/427 BC - 348/347 BC), and Aristotle (348 BC - 322 BC) play a critical role in both psychology and philosophy. In ancient Greek, philosophers would discuss many topics that now fall under the discipline of psychology, including free will vs. determinism, memory, nature vs. nurture, and more.

A little more on Psychology and how it evolved:

The early days of psychology were pretty primitive. Two dominant theoretical perspectives regarding how the brain works took hold. Namely, structuralism and functionalism. Structuralism was pioneered by Wilhelm Wundt (1832-1929). The main focus of this approach was breaking down mental processes into the most basic components. It relied on trained introspection, a research method whereby subjects related what was going on in their minds while performing specific tasks. This method proved highly ineffective because there was too much individual variation in the experiences and reports of research subjects. Functionalism, developed by an American psychologist known as William James (1842-1910), opposed structuralism.

James argued that the mind is constantly changing, and it's pointless to look for the structure of conscious experience. Instead, he proposed the focus should be on how and why an organism does something, i.e., the functions or purpose of the brain. James suggested that psychologists should look for the underlying cause of the behavior and the mental processes involved. This emphasis on the cause and consequences of behavior has influenced contemporary psychology. It forms the basis of our approach when reading and analyzing others.

Since those early days, psychology has evolved and taken on new perspectives and dimensions. Sigmund Freud's psychoanalysis was the original psychodynamic theory. Still, the psychodynamic approach as a whole includes all theories that were based on his ideas as well as other great psychologists of that time, including Erikson and Jung. This phase of psychology is often referred to as classic psychology that focuses on behaviorism. The third wave of psychology came into activation more recently that's human-centric, which brought to bear the importance of subjective experience and personal growth. As recent as the 1960s and 70s, psychology began a cognitive revolution adopting a rigorous scientific lab-based scientific approach with application to memory, perception, cognitive development, mental illness, and more.

"Psychological scientists demonstrated that organisms have innate dispositions and that human brains are distinctively prepared for diverse higher-level mental activities, from language acquisitions to mathematics as well as spatial perception, thinking, and memory. They also developed and tested diverse theoretical models for conceptualizing mental representations in complex information processing conducted at multiple levels of awareness. They asked questions as How does the individual's stored knowledge give rise to the patterns or networks of mental representations activated at a particular time? How is memory organized? In a related direction, the analysis of visual perception took increasing account of how the features of the environment (e.g., the objects, places, and other animals in one's world) provide information about the possibilities and dangers of the environment, on the one side and the animal's dispositions and adaptation efforts, on the other, become inseparable: their interactions become the focus of research and theory building. Concurrently, to investigate personality, individual differences, and social behavior, several theorists made learning these theories more social (interpersonal) and cognitive. They moved far beyond the earlier conditioning and reward-and-punishment principles, focusing on how a person's characteristics interact with situational opportunities and demands. Research demonstrated the importance of learning through observation from real and symbolic models, showing that it occurs spontaneously and cognitively without requiring any direct reinforcement."

(https://www.britannica.com/science/psychology/Impact-and-aftermath-of-the-cognitive-revolution)

Importance of psychology when reading people

The basis of friendships or relationships is interaction and understanding. A proper connection is built on trust, which relies on transparency and authenticity. To be deemed transparent and authentic, you must have a good command of yourself in every way. You must be an open book and relatable to the person you seek to establish a connection with. The other person will naturally feel like they can trust you when common ground is established. Psychology empowers us with tools and knowledge to quickly identify and leverage the common attributes that can connect us. Through psychological techniques, you will get to know and note vulnerable points or boundaries that the other person possesses so that, as you interrelate, you'll understand what grounds to tread on and not. It's all about getting to know more about someone's behaviors, traits, or even personality so that you can handle them or conduct yourself better when interacting with them.

Psychology also helps you know what to say, where, around whom, and how to say it best. It also enables you to read the clues of how your communication has been received. For example, we know that a dog wags its tail when it's happy. That's a scientifically proven study, so if a neighbor's dog comes up to you wagging its tail, then you can deduce it is very pleasing to see you. The same can apply to human interactions. People are always giving off clues in the form of reactions or traits that reveal their inner motives, intentions, or how they feel about your communication. The last thing I find psychology helps with is developing our self-confidence. When you can build up your "self," it becomes easier to handle any situation, and you learn to trust your own judgment. Analyzing people is a balance between collecting external data from the other person and having the skill and confidence to sort through that data and come to a logical conclusion. If you suffer from low self-confidence, it's going to be hard to believe in your deductions. That voice of doubt will keep diluting and sabotaging even your best efforts at reading people.

Self-confidence is enhanced when you trust your senses and firmly know what you can handle and what's true for you. Believing in yourself is a prerequisite for effective communication. How can you possibly decipher, understand or even identify other people's behavior if yours feels out of control? How can you analyze others without negative biases if you're drowning in low self-esteem and low confidence? Psychology can help you work on yourself and learn more about people, their behaviors, and why they do what they do.

How behaviors develop

There are countless theories associated with human behavior and various types of conduct. Understanding human behavior is critical in society and in our quest to analyze people, but don't be fooled. This isn't a topic that can easily be covered in a single book. For the sake of simplicity, let's refer to human behavior as the manner and reasons behind people's actions. Behavior is something that evolves as an individual goes through life. Some traits and mannerisms are inborn (you inherit them from your parents), and some are acquired through the environment and social conditioning. Most of us don't realize that behaviors can be developed and nurtured over time, much like personalities. I like to consider behavior as a manual that's encrypted in someone's mind that causes them to react or behave in a certain way concerning their circumstances or surrounding. We all possess that invisible manual, which influences all our decisions, choices, and personality. The most common theories around behavior are classic conditioning, operant conditioning, and cognition. Classical conditioning occurs when a person associates specific stimuli with various outcomes. For example, suppose you are more successful when you follow your own instincts instead of following rules that others have set. In that case, you're likely to become a nonconformist and take risks. Operant conditioning controls behavior via positive or negative reinforcement. For example, a student who regularly studies for exams and aces them comes to associate studying with positive grades. They are more likely to keep doing that. Cognition is a theory that maintains that human behavior is determined by an individual's thoughts, inner judgment, personal motivations, etc.

As we will learn in the next chapter, how people behave is primarily impacted by their personalities. Some people are patient and easy-going, while others are impatient and hot-headed. You can't tell someone's personality in an instant. It takes time and observation, but you might start catching a glimpse of who they really are through behavior. People tend to develop their behaviors as they approach different challenges and interact with their surroundings. In other words, they are influenced by what goes on around them. Suppose one is born into a family where physical abuse is a common occurrence. In that case, their behavior will somehow reflect that, either by making that person more aggressive or extraordinarily passive and indifferent.

Factors that affect behavior

• Age

Age is probably one of the most apparent factors because a young person will behave very differently compared to a senior elder. Behaviors vary with different stages and phases in life. As one gets older, we typically see more mature traits and "adult-like" behavior. You would expect particular body language cues to come from a teenage girl, but if the same reaction is observed in a fifty-year-old woman, that's a red flag.

• Environment

One's environment plays a critical role in shaping mannerisms. Things openly done tend to become engrained as the standard operating system for individuals. Perhaps a young man grew up in a household where his dad constantly berated all women in the house (the mother, babysitter, and older sister). The young man might habitually yell at waitresses, calling them incompetent and rude just because he spent so much time in an environment where women were not respected.

Can you determine behavior from communication style?

Understanding communication styles is an excellent strategy for interpreting who people are in general. Although communication styles are highly connected to an individual's personality, they also cue us into the person's dominant behavior. Typically, you will also notice specific non-verbal signals that correlate to each dominant behavior. We will dissect the most common below.

Assertive behavior

With this kind of behavior, the communication is direct. The person tends to come across as confident in who they are and what they have to say. You should note that this type of person will not disregard or belittle your opinions while conversing. They will understand and value your unique perspective. Still, they will clarify that they stand on their own beliefs and cannot be seduced into abandoning what they value. This type of communication style is considered one of the most effective methods for interacting with others, especially if one is a leader.

Suppose you were interacting with a person and a misunderstanding occurred. You'd observe that an assertive person would openly speak their mind, after which they might cue you in (with their eyes, a nod, or through their voice) to also speak your mind. In terms of body language signals, an assertive person would use a friendly gaze while you talk to show they are attentive. They tend to use smiling, nodding, and other encouraging body signals to express themselves. We call their body language "Inclusive" because it projects calmness, openness, and collaboration. Such individuals are unlikely to make rapid and vigorous hand movements. Assertive people exhibit behavior that causes others to feel comfortable, heard, and valued.

Aggressive behavior

Aggressive behavior in an individual is often characterized by this overwhelming need to win. The people to exhibit aggressive behavior do so to intimidate and have their way with others. They are often quite hostile and threatening. Their verbal and non-verbal communication is what we refer to as "conclusive" because they generally disregard the opinions and thoughts of others. Only what they say and think matters. You will observe harsh tones, vigorous hand movements, increased volume, furrowed eyebrows, a clenched jaw, and at times temper tantrums coming from the other person. Be on the lookout for facial expressions and facial movements that disregard others. Check for that attitude of being unwilling to embrace any different opinions or ideas. Suppose you notice that someone is unnecessarily agitated and leaking hostile emotions or showing signs of conflict. In that case, you're dealing with an aggressive personality type.

Passive behavior

People pleasers tend to have passive behavior. This type of communication is commonly referred to as submissive communication. Passive communicators are unable to authentically express themselves. Even when they have great ideas that could help matters, they would rather keep quiet and go by what others say. Some call them pushovers because of how passive they are and the fact that their body language is very stagnant. It's easy to assume all is well with this type of person when in fact, they might be struggling or suffering. Over time, however, this type of person tends to become resentful. The most common signal you'll notice from such a person is how silent they are. This individual never wants to share their insight. They might sit in the back of the room in utter silence throughout the meeting. You might notice that even if a conflict or misunderstanding occurs, this person will do everything possible to avoid confrontation. The only strategy they rely on when communicating is silence.

Passive-Aggressive behavior

Sometimes you'll come across a personality that combines both passive and aggressive behavior. In such cases, you end up with a passive-aggressive style of communication. That means, on the surface, the person will come across as silent and submissive, sweet and pleasing. But underneath their actions, there's brewing anger and resentment. Such individuals might smile in your presence and immediately gossip or demean you when you leave the room.

A friend of mine is married to a passive-aggressive woman. They might be at a friend's BBQ, and she'll walk up to a high school friend, smile, and chat for a while then, as soon as they walk away, she might turn to her husband and say all kinds of awful things about her so-called "high school friend." This is just one example of how passive-aggressive behavior presents itself. Unlike people with aggressive behavior, these individuals are not open and honest about their true feelings.

To identify a passive-aggressive person, you need to check for seemingly reserved character traits often masked by sentiments that reflect negative thoughts. Often they will use eye contact, silence, and space to convey their passive-aggressive behavior.

Manipulative behavior

People with this type of behavior will use tricks and deceit to convince others and get their way. Manipulative people do not disclose their real intentions and tend to be insincere and condescending. You can quickly identify manipulative behavior by being mindful of a person's body language and noticing when there's a disconnect between their words and actions. But the best way to identify this type of behavior and personality is through understanding dark psychology.

Positive psychology and dark psychology: what's the difference?

Just as we know that electricity can give life or take life, so can psychological knowledge. Most psychological knowledge is used for good. In fact, positive psychology is a branch that mainly focuses on the positive events and influences in life, like the things that make life worth living. All topics studied under this field, including life satisfaction, happiness, well-being, self-confidence, and more, help people live their best lives. But there's also the dark side of psychology, and some people have studied it with ill intentions. If you think about many of the great bullies, dictators, and ruthless leaders in our history (e.g., Hilter, Stalin, and many more), you'll realize that these individuals could manipulate the masses because they understood psychology. Even the best serial killers and other criminals tend to be masters of psychology. They use their skills and knowledge in dark ways. In recent years, the term dark psychology has become a real thing and its own field of study. Its primary focus is learning the art of manipulation and mind control. Dark psychology is a term that references when people use tactics of coercion, manipulation, persuasion, and motivation to get what they want from others.

In fact, the term "Dark Triad" is huge within the field of dark psychology, and it refers to narcissists, Machiavellians, and psychopaths. Narcissists are self-centered, lack empathy, and usually have enormous egos and a sense of grandiosity. Machiavellians exploit and deceive others (especially those they feel are weak) with no sense of morality. Psychopaths tend to come off as friendly and charming, but, deep down, they are impulsive, selfish, and remorseless, lack empathy, and enjoy inflicting pain on others.

These personality traits are very destructive in society, especially when the individual in question has no intention of changing. All these personalities rely heavily on manipulating others to get what they want. But I'm getting ahead of myself here. Let's focus on personalities and how you can get better at deciphering them in the next chapter.

Chapter 06: Personality Types

Human awareness is very limited, at least for the majority of us. What gets your attention also prevents you from seeing the whole picture. The objects you don't expect often go unnoticed while your attention is focused on what you expect. It's normal for us to subconsciously ignore specific facts, data, and knowledge because of our conditioning and limited observation skills. Growing evidence suggests that personality traits affect our experience of the world and shape the course of our lives. In other words, your personality affects how you perceive reality and determines your choices in life. The same is true for any other person in your world. A psychological study by Antinori, Carter & Smillie revealed that open-minded people may live in a completely different reality. They found that creativity, perception, and overall world experience will differ depending on one's mood and openness. But what exactly is personality?

What is personality?

There are varying definitions for this complex term. "Personality is defined as the character sets of behaviors, cognitions, and emotional patterns that evolve from biological and environmental factors" (Wikipedia). Britannica takes a different angle to define personality, stating that it is "a characteristic way of thinking, feeling, and behaving." Personality as a term has its origins in the Greek word *Persona*, which translates to a theatrical mask worn by performers to either project roles or disguise their identities. We can at least agree that personality is a combination of moods, attitudes, opinions, and behaviors and that it's mostly expressed and visible during interactions with other people.

In other words, unless someone is interacting with you for a significant period, you have no way of identifying their personality.

What makes up a personality?

Consistency is one of the characteristics of personality. Meaning that you can recognize a repeating pattern in that individual if you watch them long enough. Essentially, we know that people act in the same ways or similar ways in various situations. They become predictable to you as an outside observer. Behaviors and actions align based on personality. For instance, someone with an aggressive personality will predictably react to his environment. Suppose you've observed this person long enough and have accurate data. In that case, you can tell how he will move and act in any given situation, especially when under stress. Personality isn't just in behavior. You can also see it expressed in a person's emotional state, how they handle their close relationships, and other social interactions. Although personality is a psychological construct, research suggests that it's also influenced by biological processes and needs. Add to that mix the natural character traits of a person and their thought patterns. You've got yourself the building blocks of a personality.

Personality Vs. Character

Lots of people trip on this because they tend to assume character and personality are synonyms. The truth is they are different. You need to discern when you're discovering someone's personality and when you're uncovering their true character. What's the difference? Personality is actually easier to read. We tend to recognize someone as optimistic, aggressive, energetic, extroverted, introverted, overly serious, pessimistic, shy, and so on. All we need to do is observe them for a little while during that first interaction. These are all personality traits that help us read the person quickly as we get to know them. Still, they don't necessarily reveal who that person is. A person's character takes time (a lot of time) to uncover. It constitutes traits that reveal themselves only in specific and often uncommon circumstances. Here we're talking about qualities like kindness, honesty, strength, and so on. Traits don't just tell you how the person carries themselves (which is often the case with personality traits). Instead, you get to know who that person really is. Can you sense the difference?

Character traits are rooted in beliefs, and although beliefs can be changed, it's a lot harder to do. We unconsciously tend to connect personality to a character for two main reasons. First, we want to like people we already like and want them to be good since we like them. The second is that assessing a person's character is laborious and time-consuming. We'd actually need to invest time with that person and observe their behavior in character-challenging situations to make reliable deductions about who they really are. Let's take an example of making a new friend at a party and seriously hoping to develop a lasting friendship with him. Then you pick up on a lie. And he lies so casually and easily, you can reasonably deduce even from that single lie that this is something he's done in the past and is likely to repeat in the future. Although you loved his personality and thought of initiating a deep friendship, the only way to know his true character (dishonest and deceptive, or was that just a fluke) would be to invest way more time solving that puzzle. The only question is, does it feel worthwhile to you? With inconclusive data about his character, you might choose to walk away and never speak after that party. That's not to say you figured out his character. Still, you did "catch" something that felt off and if it doesn't align with your values, then stepping away from such a personality is best.

Wouldn't it be great if you could somehow catch these hidden beliefs that are often disguised by personality traits?

Well, it turns out you can! You may not get to the heart of a person's character or catch their beliefs by speaking directly to that individual, but you can uncover more of their character by speaking with those who know that individual's character. This is why you'll find many employers asking to speak to a reference. And when you talk to someone who knows that person well enough, ask questions designed to get them to reveal their most accurate judgments honestly. For example, "What, in your judgment, is [name]'s greatest weakness?" Do your best to read between the lines when the answer is given. Also, make sure you're using this technique on someone with sound judgment. If you can ask multiple people this question, even better because that gives you enough data to contrast and compare with your own analysis.

The spectrum of all personality types and personality traits

Personalities vary from person to person. Many even have multiple personalities (like having different masks that you can swap at will), which they express depending on the situation. There are type theories—the early perspectives we learned regarding personalities that suggested personality types are related to biological influences. There are also trait theories, which view personality as the result of internal characteristics. Let's focus on the latter.

Trait theories

• Open
Openness as a personality trait is expressed as a sense of transparency and fluidity. An open person tends to have fewer boundaries and is very free with life. You might notice the person is quite ambitious and perhaps adventurous, always eager to grasp new ideas and curious about everything. They are often willing to go the extra mile to learn something new and possess a functional and effective sense of imagination. They often create possibilities and different approaches in handling issues.

Such individuals come across as appreciative, warm, welcoming, and feels like an open book. Some of them also exhibit traits such as being easy-going and quick to read and analyze.

• Extrovert
Extroverted personalities tend to also be very open, especially for those who are outgoing. Social butterflies is another name for this type of personality. They are always mingling, socializing, and seeking new adventures and stimulation. An extrovert is often bubbly, very talkative, and has a way with people. They communicate naturally well and knows how to build rapport and connections with the people they interact with. Most of the time, extroverts are just born that way. They perfect it over time as they develop into "the life of the party" wherever they go (high school, college, workplace, family reunions, etc.). But it can also be developed

over time if you have the patience and belief in your ability to express this personality trait.

Observing this personality in motion, you might notice that the individual likes to make things easier for others and hold the conversations around them. They tend to bring people together and come across as light-hearted, easy-going, acceptable, and easily adaptable.

• Introvert
Introverts are reserved, thoughtful, passive, and prefer to lead private lives. They are most comfortable interacting in small groups and need alone time to reset and recharge themselves. Introverts prefer quiet environments and focus on their inner thoughts and ideas instead of what's happening externally. Carl Jung was among the first psychologists to use the terms introvert and extroverts (also spelled extraverts) in the 1920s. Jung said the main difference between introverts and extroverts is that introverts turn to their own minds for stimulation and recharge.

In contrast, extroverts seek the same by looking to others to fulfill their energy needs. Although a third of all the people in the U.S are introverts, they are not all possessing identical traits. A study showed that introverts tend to fall into four subtypes.

Social introverts. This personality type is a classic introvert. He or she likes small groups and prefers quiet settings over crowds all the time.

Thinking introverts. This personality is more of a daydreamer. Such an individual spends most of their wakeful time in their mind imagining things and thinking creatively.

Anxious introverts. This personality type is ever anxious, worried, and concerned. They prefer to be along as much as possible because they feel shy and awkward being around people.

Inhibited introverts. This personality type is very restrained and struggles with decision-making because they need time to think through everything. Getting a simple yes or no out of such a person is painstaking. Although an introvert can switch over time from one sub-category to another or perhaps even become less of an introvert as they go through life, it's unlikely that an introvert can switch to an extrovert.

• Conscientious
Personalities who are conscientious tend to be "serious" in their mannerisms. They are thoughtful, goal-oriented, and have plenty of self-control. Such individuals are likely organized and prefer to move and work according to an outlined priority. They always feel obliged to get things done in a particular order, even if it means going out of their way. In other words, they take their responsibility very seriously and don't bode well with people who don't understand or recognize this. Most of the time, you'll find low-key leaders with strong ethics possessing this type of personality. Discipline and high levels of

self-control are common in this personality type, and they rarely get distracted or easily swayed from their priorities. In observation, you'll notice this person comes across more like the "go-to" person or the responsible one in the group that everyone depends on, and they quite enjoy being perceived as such.

• Agreeable
That doesn't mean one is a "yes man," but it does mean one cares about others, feels empathy are genuinely enjoys helping others.

It's almost impossible to get into confrontation or disagreement with such a person because they are just so nice! Most of the time, agreeable personalities tend to be quite open-minded, making them come across as kind, calm and composed. They have a helping heart that's always willing to go beyond the limits of the situation just for your happiness. I'm telling you, this is the kind of personality you want to find whenever you have a complaint in a store or need a late checkout at your hotel. You can be rude and harsh with them all you want, but you won't break such a person. People with such traits are so devoted to creating happiness in others that they can self-sacrifice. That's why these personality types are so appealing to narcissists and other manipulators. They are quick to trust and slow to abandon even the people who hurt them.

In observation, you'll notice a calm, peaceful, agreeable nature that is quite rare. They are likable, sociable, forgiving, and extremely loyal.

- Neurotic

Neurotics are like a ticking time bomb, if you ask me. One wrong choice and things become disastrous. The line between peace and a mental meltdown is very thin, so exercise caution when interacting with such individuals. Most skeptics fall into this category of personality. These people rarely believe in luck and question everything. They also worry about everything that happens and tend to overthink, analyze, redo and undo things when they're not satisfied (which is most of the time). If the personality is left unchecked, it's easy for a neurotic person to spiral down into depression and chronic anxiety, leading to mental health issues.

Personality Types in detail

- The Composed

As the name suggests, this personality type appears very composed all the time. They might come across as quiet and shy (a bit introverted) in the first encounter, but as they warm up and become familiar with you, things change. You might notice a shift in how approachable, spontaneous and open-minded they become. Such individuals believe in adding value to themselves and those they interact with. Although they are quiet and have no problem keeping to themselves, they are not necessarily introverted. In fact, they enjoy exploring new grounds, experimenting with new things, exchanging ideas, and imparting wisdom once they feel comfortable around you. These individuals tend to be inventors and ideologists in our society. One of the main traits you might pick up is their quiet, introverted side. They will listen more than they talk and won't necessarily socialize if you're in a party or group. You'll notice they prefer to think and reflect in silence instead of loudly voicing their opinion, even in a meeting room. Another aspect that stands out is that they tend to be quite sensitive and keenly aware of their environment. Because they are observant, they notice the details that others might miss. They are very in tune with their feelings and openly say they rely on their "gut instinct" to make the right decision.

• The visionary
The visionary personality type is rare in our society. That's because as much as they are extraverted, they tend to prefer to big talk on futuristic accomplishments and things they deem meaningful. Small talk is one of their peeves, and they cannot stand interactions or conversations that don't challenge their thinking or reasoning. Finding like-minded people is one of the things they desire, which isn't always easy, especially in certain environments. Mental stimulation drives such a person. It won't take long for you to realize you're interacting with a visionary, even if it's the first meeting.

You'll notice the individual is authoritative, intelligent, confident, and highly knowledgeable of certain key issues. They are very detail-oriented and concise in their facts and the ideas they share. Their approach to information is logical and objective.

They aren't interested in voicing opinions for the sake of argument but, at the same time, won't hesitate to question issues that do not satisfy their mental state. Most visionaries are extroverted and enjoy being around people so they can feed their minds with knowledge. They enjoy getting into highly stimulating conversations and debates. Visionaries are also highly intuitive and have a high sense of imagination. It helps them see things from a three-sixty degree perspective, uncovering information the average person wouldn't notice. When it comes to decision-making, they trust their instincts even more than their mind. Thinking is, however, one of the things they excel at. They prefer big thinking and have no difficulty telling it like it is, even if the truth is uncomfortable. While they aren't aggressive or obnoxious, they prefer to rely on logic and facts when dealing with others. They would rather speak the raw truth than sugarcoat it with facts just to spare another's feelings.

• The nurturer

This personality type is considered very selfless, giving, and generous. They think more of others than themselves and like to invest their time nurturing and growing people, ideas, projects, and more. Once the person believes in something, they will uphold it and believe in its ability with enthusiasm. Such an individual will come across as warm, welcoming, philanthropic, and open to embracing new people and ideas. You'll also notice a particular sensitivity with this personality, especially regarding feelings and emotions. These individuals prefer collaboration to competition. They believe in giving their all, especially when something leads to a greater good. They like being part of something bigger than their individual needs, and they can be an excellent catalyst for success and progress.

When it comes to their personality traits, you'll tend to find this particular personality to be quite introverted, reserved, and quiet despite their openness. When exchanging information, this type of person needs time, and you must give them time to process things fully on their own. Think of them as quiet thinkers who are good with others but also require time on their own to reset, reflect and recharge. Their sensitivity to emotions makes them very empathetic and attuned to their immediate environment. While it serves them well to be present and pragmatic, they tend not to care about the future or abstract ideas. In decision-making, these individuals rely more on their hearts than logic and believe in doing what's right for the greater good of all. They tend to self sacrifice their own needs in service of others, but that doesn't mean they are submissive. In fact, these people are very strategic, disciplined, well organized, and always strive to know the facts before making any judgments. They like following a routine-based program that can keep them accountable while at the same time nurturing the people or relationships they value.

- The thinker

You may view the thinker as the brains behind all the institutions, ideas, or corporations that you know.

Their personality type is smart, complex, creative, and innovative. It's rather hard to put into words how you would know you're in the presence of a thinker, but suffice it to say, you would know. Their personality is so rare, and they have a natural ability to read people and situations super fast, so if you spend a few minutes with someone who feels like they already analyzed you and can predict your every move, then it's likely you've encountered this personality. One of their main traits is the fact that they enjoy being alone. They are very self-sufficient and prefer to seclude themselves to recharge and refresh their brain. These individuals find comfort in solidarity and do their best thinking when left alone. Their creative juices are constantly flowing, which makes their imagination extremely powerful. While others shy away from challenging thoughts and complexities, these personality types seek out complexities to decipher and simplify them. Compared to the nurturer, we can surmise that these personality types are more future-oriented. They prefer to bring the ideas in their minds to life than engage with present matters or relationships. A thinker primarily leads with his head, not his heart, making him highly factual and intellectual. Some call these people "whiz kids," "geniuses," etc. Regardless of the name you choose to use, the things that make them stand out are their highly advanced mental abilities and the ease with which they master their chosen topic.

- The commander

The commander personality type is an inborn leader who can garner respect based on their actions and behavior. They can be a little egocentric and carry a sense of entitlement to rule and tower above everyone else. Still, as long as it's in healthy doses, it doesn't become destructive. The healthy versions of this personality won't go around with pumped-up chests, but their presence naturally brings forth this air of authority. These individuals are highly intuitive and have excellent judgment and reasoning. They look at things through their lens of authority and enjoy taking charge and leading the way, even in dangerous circumstances. If you're familiar with the term "alpha," you already have a basic understanding of how this personality portrays itself. Most of the time, this personality will be extraverted and easily approachable. They radiate natural leadership qualities, and they crave conquest and adventure. The commander finds pleasure in exploring new grounds, facing challenges, and being at the forefront of it all.

Although they aren't the best listeners and prefer to give than take advice, they do pay attention to the counsel of those they trust. Their highly intuitive nature enables them to think outside the box and consider both facts and gut instincts before deciding. They have strong wills, high self-esteem, and believe in their judgment more than most. Being organized is a vital skill these individuals possess. They know how to keep their weaknesses in check and rally people behind their ideas. They are protocol-oriented and rarely act impulsively. Decision-making is critical for these individuals. They like to come across as bold, decisive, and clear-minded, so they work hard to train themselves into effective decision-makers. Their joy is to stand out as dominant, reliable, and ever ready for whatever life throws their way.

• The craftsman
This personality type is very logical. They view themselves as highly rational beings. In observation, this personality type is typically hard to decipher and quite mysterious. They tend to be quite unpredictable and seem to change over time. You can never know their next move or plan or even what they are really thinking. They tend to have a poker face on most of the time, and it takes a highly skilled master communicator and people analyzer to get an accurate read of such a personality. When it comes to their work, life, and relationships, they are very detail-oriented, open-minded, and believe in equality. Many are introverted, choosing to seclude themselves from the masses most of the time because they feel that too much interaction diminishes their energy and distorts their thinking patterns. By default, they tend to be highly sensitive and aware of their surroundings. They are also fairly observant, trying to get the complete picture in any given situation. Craftsmen are brainy (not as intellectual as the thinker) but certainly likes to sit and ponder, create and analyze. They mostly enjoy fixing things and making things right. That's why this personality might be attracted to relationships that are bad for

him in an attempt to repair the other person and bring perspectives back where he feels they should be. One of the things they value is freedom in creativity, expression, and in life. They do not believe in rules or matters that affect or constrict them of their desire to flourish.

Reading personality types

Now that we've identified personality and explored various personality traits, it's time to put your people analysis into practice. In this section, we'll start creating different buckets of personality and see how you can start reading the people around you depending on the traits you identify.

Are you extroverted or introverted?

Although there are many theories to read personalities, let's go with the simplest one. There are four main categories, and within each are two personalities. A good starting place is to identify whether the person you're interacting with is introverted or extroverted. An introvert will speak calmly (at times very quietly and slowly), withdraws from the spotlight, and avoids being the center of attention. You'll notice the person doesn't talk much and tends to linger on one topic for an extended period of time. Extroverts, on the other hand, are loud. They talk a lot and with a lot of enthusiasm in their voice. They can talk about a variety of topics within a matter of minutes and seem to keep jumping from one topic to the next in a very short time. This person seems to know everyone and likes to be friends with everyone around them.

Once you've identified which bucket the person falls into, it's time to pick up on how sensitive or intuitive they are.

Are you sensor or more intuitive?

About one-third of the population is predominantly intuitive. That means most of the people we encounter will be sensors. Although you might not pick this up through analyzing someone within a few minutes, you should be on the lookout for clues that help you figure out whom you're dealing with. Sensors, being the majority tend to relate through their five senses (hence the name). They predominantly run their lives based on what they can physically process and comprehend. So they will come across as more realistic, practical, factual, and focused on the past and the present. Most of their information is based on experience and what the senses can prove. Intuitive people, on the other hand, are dreamers. They are highly imaginative, run their lives predominantly on ideas, the future, and theory. Their focus is mainly on the future and seems to care very little about what has passed. They believe the senses are too limiting and bounding to be trusted. They struggle to understand how the rest of the people can lead such limited livelihoods. It would be easy to pick up through words and body movement whether someone experiences the world through their senses or intuition. Just observe them carefully long enough.

Are you a thinker or a feeler?

The next bucket is determining whether you're dealing with someone who is logical and only relies on their head for decision making, or one who is more emotionally attuned. As a general rule of thumb, we tend to assume men are thinkers and women are feelers. But as with all things, this is an oversimplification, because we find a minority of men who are predominantly feelers (a third of the male population) and a minority of women (also a third of the population) who are thinkers. Thinkers generally exude high levels of confidence, and they prefer to deal with facts. They are very goal-oriented and usually don't take things personally, even if you hold an opposing point of view. Feelers are more emotional and tend to take things personally. They believe it's more important to be liked and to help others instead of pursuing selfing goals. It's easier to get a feeler to open up about their thoughts and emotions, and they value love, peace, and "getting along" far more than thinkers.

If you're wondering where to place someone, start noticing what the person is more receptive to. Are they opening up more when you're logical and emphasizing goal achievement? Do they frequently imply how much they value honesty, truth, and justice? Are they comfortable offering their judgment and opinions even if they know you won't agree? If so, you're probably dealing with a thinker.

On the other hand, you'll notice that a feeler is very personal, friendly, and has no problem opening up about themselves. You'll notice how much the person pays attention to the people around them and how helpful they are. In their words and non-verbal cues, you'll pick up the vibe of peace, love, and creating harmony around everything they do. For example, I once got invited to lunch by an old friend who thought it might be a good idea if I met his new business partner. A few minutes after sitting at the restaurant, I could tell this guy was a rare gem. He was very friendly, took extra care to make sure we were comfortable, and that I liked this restaurant which was supposedly his pick. As the waitress came, he was extremely polite and inquired about her sickly mother. During our lunch meeting, he regularly included phrases like "we must work together" and "it's critical for the team to feel cared for and valued." These are a few signals that let you know the person is a feeler.

Are you contrived or spontaneous?

One more category to discern as early on as possible is whether the person is contrived or spontaneous. Contrived individuals tend to also be perfectionists, which is great because they are very organized, detail-oriented, and hold themselves to high standards. Still, it also brings a lot of drawbacks. These individuals are serious and often maintain a strict schedule. There's a never-ending checklist that runs their lives. Although they are good at planning and time management, they always seem to be in a rush. Spontaneous personalities are, of course, the opposite. Being organized isn't something they do well. They are open, flexible and while they might make a plan, they rarely follow it. This can create some procrastination and poor time-management issues, but it's a great personality to foster creativity. In observation, you'll find a contrived personality to be quite serious, opinionated, judgemental, clean, organized, and great at sticking to a schedule or plan. Many leaders tend to fall into this category. A spontaneous personality might come across as messy, disorganized, and too easy-going. Still, they are undoubtedly fun to be around. They are light-hearted and highly creative and open-minded.

How to tell a person's personality type fast

Although we are told never to judge a book by its cover, that's precisely what we need to start with. After all, first impressions do matter. So the first thing to notice is the person's appearance. How a person presents themselves to the world (little-to-no grooming or excellent grooming practices) tells us a lot about them. A person who takes care of themselves will practice basic hygiene. They will wear nice clothes, and that will have an impact on their level of confidence. The clothes they are wearing and any artifacts can also tell you a little bit more about them. Go back to the chapter where we discussed emblems and artifacts if you're unsure about how to interpret this. The next thing to note is their posture. Suppose the person is slouching and barely making any eye contact. In that case, it could be that they are uncomfortable in that environment or lacking self-confidence. It could be an indication that the person is either an introvert or a highly sensitive individual. Keep collecting data to figure out which it is.

You might also want to pay attention to the words they use, their paralinguistic signals, and the emotions that leak as they speak. A person who likes to use sophisticated and complex words might think himself important and intellectual, and therefore wants to show off how impressive he is. If they talk a lot and keep interrupting you, then you can be sure they are extroverted.

Aside from the non-verbal cues, you should also ask plenty of questions to get the person talking about themselves so you can learn more about their interests, job, and worldview. What someone is interested in can clue you in about their personality. For example, suppose you're at a party; you just got introduced to a guy who barely speaks a word for half an hour. So you pose a friendly question and get a conversation going. It becomes evident that he's not a big talker and doesn't like the spotlight on him. Before concluding that he's an extroverted, highly sensitive individual, gather a bit more intel by learning more about his hobbies. Suppose he says he enjoys spending hours alone writing poetry or coding programs in his basement. In that case, it's likely your first impression was correct. You wouldn't expect someone like that to say he enjoys extreme sports or going to live football matches every weekend. The more questions you can ask to understand a person's daily life and worldview, the easier it will be to make sense of the data you've collected through initial observation.

Understanding what drives people

Our behavior is often influenced by a combination of internal and/or external factors. Internal (or "push") motivation is a biological driving factor that originates from within. It's more about meeting survival instincts, such as the need to have food, water, and sex; it could also be the drive to fulfill a psychological need. External or "pull" motivation comes from our environment. It can include social approval, acceptance, the need to achieve, and the motivation to take or avoid risks.

Personality theory and research suggest that people are motivated in different ways depending on personality traits. A high level of a specific trait will often cause individuals to act as the attribute implies. The "trait-environment correlation studies" show that if we exhibit characteristics at one end of a personality dimension, we will seek out, create or modify situations differently than the individuals at the other end of the spectrum. It will also impact the goals we choose and what we prioritize. For example, an extrovert and an introvert might react similarly to stimuli designed to put them in a pleasant hedonic mood. Still, you will notice a significant difference with the extraverts when there's a desirable reward because they react with greater energetic arousal in response to the pursuit of rewards and are more likely than introverts to seek social stimulation in a variety of situations (Deckers,2014).

Herbert L.Petri of Towson University has published online documentation of his intensive studies to uncover the four main drivers of behavior. In his publication, he says that after 35 years of research, he believes four major components act and interact to produce motivated behavior: biology, environment, cognition, and emotions. Let's give an overview of each.

We already touched on biology, which many psychologists claim plays a critical role in behavior.

Although the study of motivated behavior from the exclusive perspective of hardwired biological commands is not as popular as it once was, what has become increasingly apparent is that biological processes, sometimes even at the level of genes, can predispose individuals to behave in particular ways (Four Motivational Components of Behavior, Herbert L. Petri).

Environment
We've talked a lot about how your upbringing influenced the kind of person you are today. The

same is true for everyone else you interact with. They learn behaviors natural to their environment, which drives how they communicate, what they focus on, and how they show up in the world. It should also be noted that biology and environment can (and often do) interact to produce behaviors such as shyness, aggressiveness, etc.

Cognition
In the last forty years, research has been ongoing to examine the role of cognition in motivation. Most of this research is centered around humans. The gist of it is that how we interpret the available information around us can influence our behavior. Imagine for a moment that you're interacting with a woman who misreads your direct tone and confidence as aggression. She will likely turn hostile and send off negative verbal and non-verbal signals as you attempt to make conversation. This is one example of how cognition works. Although we may be predisposed to interpret information in a particular way, it is also true that learning plays a crucial role in our understanding.

We are not born with the expectation that particular food will taste good, but we quickly learn and remember the ones that do. We are also likely to make attributions in a specific situation based on memories of experiences that were learned earlier. Those experiences may have resulted from parings of events (classical conditioning), pleasant or unpleasant outcomes (instrumental conditioning), or the observation of others (observational learning).

Emotions

From an evolutionary standpoint, the ability to act as a result of emotion, almost automatically and with little or no higher cognitive processing, was advantageous, especially in potentially dangerous situations when there wasn't enough time to process information through rational thinking. Research on the neural circuitry of emotion (LeDoux, 1994, 1996, 2000) has provided strong evidence for the role of several cell groups within the amygdala in emotions. LeDoux (2000) provided evidence for circuity that would allow sensory input to trigger emotion directly without higher cortical processing suggesting that semi-autonomous emotional circuits play a critical role in motivating behavior.

We may not live in hostile and life-threatening environments now, but this research is still valid. It gives us insight into why someone who barely knows you might send off non-verbal signals that don't seem to make sense. Let me illustrate with a basic example.

During a boy's night out, I was introduced to my buddy's girlfriend, who happened to come out with a few of her work colleagues. One of the girls kept sending me mixed signals. I'd met her once before at a networking event. We exchanged a few words but nothing more. Later in the night, when I felt it appropriate, I approached her to better understand why she seemed somewhat hostile toward me. After a few drinks and well-calibrated questions, she finally opened up. She revealed that she'd heard a rumor from some girls in her WhatsApp group that I was selfish, promiscuous, and, in short, a jerk around women. The non-verbal signals finally made sense, to my satisfaction; the look of disgust and contempt matched the information she gave me. Of course, it didn't sit well with me that she thought ill of me based on hyperbolized information. So I did my best to try and convince her otherwise. The point of this story is to show you how emotions can drive behavior. Everything that lady did that night and the signals she sent were all driven by her feelings of disdain and disapproval of me. I caught wind of it and sought answers which enabled me to clear the air and win her over to my side. The bottom line is that we are always driven by something, whether it's an emotional, a biological need, or something else. By identifying the underlying driving factor, you can influence the conversation and the person more successfully.

Rules to help you read others:

Here's the thing. If you make the wrong assumption in your analysis, you've essentially lost even before you begin. Many heated fights, lost sales, and broken hearts are caused by a few critical errors. That might seem like an oversimplification again. Perhaps it's not right to break down human behavior into rules and categories. Still, despite how complex we are as humans, we tend to be fairly predictable.

A lot of our behavior happens unconsciously, on autopilot, so maybe there is a way to systematize how we analyze people based on some of the repetitive behavior that's now scientifically proven. I learned about these four rules to understanding what makes people tick. After applying it for the better part of a decade, I really do think it's a great strategy for anyone to use when reading people. So let me share with you my approach.

One. I assume that everyone cares more about themselves than me.

If you think people are thinking about you, then you're wrong. In reality, the only person who thinks about you a lot is you. Studies show that sixty percent of our thoughts are self-directed. Only thirty percent are relationship-based (e.g., What does she think of me? Will my boss finally give me that raise?), and a meager ten percent are empathy-driven, i.e., you're spending time thinking through the perspective of another person. So if you're sitting there reading someone and getting all puffed up by the fact that they are not extending that warm invitation, trust me, that's you reading too much into the situation. It could be that the person is introverted and doesn't feel courageous enough to initiate. Maybe they are praying you'll be the bigger man. Most of the time, this is the case.

Two. People are almost always driven by selfish altruism.

Now we're getting at the heart of why anyone does what they do. It would be misleading to assume that everyone always acts out of selfish needs, as that doesn't account for the helpful personalities willing to self-sacrifice in the name of a greater good. There's a better way of approaching this topic that seems to cover all corners of why we do what we do. Let's call it selfish altruism. People do nice things as a way to feel good about themselves or to get what they want, and this isn't a bad thing. Researchers who study primates noticed the same thing happens even within the animal kingdom. They discovered four primary categories of selfish altruism: dominance, reciprocity, trade, and familial.

Familial - is helping those who share your genes. It makes sense from an evolutionary perspective that we would favor those we feel are just like us. Primates do this and so do humans.

Reciprocity - is about giving back to the one who gave you something, either directly or indirectly. In other words, you scratch my back; I'll scratch yours. This concept of reciprocity is extremely powerful in humans. In his book, Robert Cialdini writes about it as one of the best ways to influence others and get what you want. Think about a time when a colleague insisted on paying for your morning Starbucks coffee or maybe picked up the tab during lunch.

Didn't you feel the overwhelming need to pay him back somehow?

Trade - is about exchanging something directly. I have beans, but I need copper, and you have plenty of copper, but you need beans. We have a common ground right there, and we can easily enter into a mutually beneficial interaction and agreement.

Dominance - is widespread and well pronounced in primates, but humans do it too (albeit in more sophisticated ways). Some primates will give help as a way of asserting dominance in the group. It's as if they are saying, "Look at how powerful I am that I can give some of my resources to help you." Truth be told, I can name family members who behave similarly.

So although humans are a bit more subtle and sophisticated in their selfish altruism, realize that majority of us are driven to act based on one or a combination of these categories. Believe it or not, most people are not looking to cheat, swindle and lie all day long to get what they want. It's wrong to assume people are uncaring and selfish in their actions. But at the same time, it's also naive and inaccurate to think people are entirely selfless in their acts. Find the middle ground as you continue to collect your data.

Three. Thinking isn't a commonplace activity, so don't assume the other person is actively thinking about each and every non-verbal signal.

Most of our day is run entirely by the subconscious programming that runs in the background. You might think someone is consciously or deliberating doing or behaving in a particular way. I can assure you unless they are part of the elite group of people working on their self-mastery and communication (like you), much of what you'll pick up is subconscious communication. This is especially the case whenever you come across someone who says one thing, but your gut instinct tells you they don't really mean it. Observe their nonverbal communication well enough, and you might just read into what's really going on. Thinking is a hard job that few are willing to partake in. Scientists estimate that more than a third of our thoughts are regurgitated or recycled. Be mindful of this as you analyze the person because they might be reacting or responding to you based on an unconscious pattern and not your words.

Four. Conformity is the standard operating system.

Many people prefer to fit in than stand out because they fear rejection or being seen as an outcast. Therefore, don't be surprised if you pick up many similarities when analyzing people who belong to the same click, group, or team. Sometimes, people will send fake messages to make it seem like they fit into a particular group. For example, you might notice two of your colleagues making the same statements. One of them will come across as more "forced" because she might be trying to be just like her team member to please the boss. Whenever you pick up some of these cues in their non-verbal communication, don't judge harshly. Remember our society values and encourages "sameness." The school system, the media, and even our parents encourage us to be like so-and-so. As a teen in high school, you see many cliques that dress, talk, and act the same to show they "belong" to that group. This doesn't change when we become adults. It morphs in various ways, but you'll start to pick it up as you observe people. Sometimes a person will behave a certain way because they are driven by the need to "fit in" or belong. If you notice this happening, continue collecting your data because, sooner or later, those outer layers do fall off.

Extensive reading of the subtle emotional cues we often give off while communicating has taught me that certain emotions are easier to pick up. Feelings like fear, anger, disgust, and contempt tend to hide in the background, but if they are driving that individual's behavior, they tend to leak out during an interaction.

If someone is fearful, you'll notice it in their eyes, lips, and neck. Eyebrows get pulled together and upwards. Lips stretch towards the ears, which causes the neck to become tense, creating vertical ridges. If the person is angry, the eyes become narrower as they communicate, and their eyebrows and lips tighten as though they are trying to contain the anger. Disgust is usually cued in by wrinkling of the nose and a raised upper lip which is often harder to spot, but you can also sense it in the tone. Contempt is another one that's had to pick up, but once you have enough cluster data, you should be able to recognize it in the face, the words used, and the tone and pitch.

Manipulative personalities (The dark triad)

In chapter five, we introduced the concept of a dark triad and how certain personalities can be manipulative. It's time to dive a little better into how people with dark personalities manipulate others and what you need to be on the lookout for.

Emotional manipulation is a technique all dark personalities employ. Instead of using positive influence, they turn to emotional manipulation and deceit to get what they want. Emotional manipulation occurs when the person seeks power over you so they can control or even victimize you.

Sometimes we fall into bad habits and poor communication, which could lead to a bit of manipulation. I doubt anyone reading this can confidently swear that they've never manipulated someone in their life to have their way. Kids do it to their parents all the time, and spouses certainly do it to each other. I could go on. What I'm getting at is that we're not talking about that once in a while "bad behavior" that we might use when having a bad day. Instead, we are talking about the perfected art some people deploy that can be considered pathological manipulation (Machiavellians and narcissists are experts). You must learn how to quickly identify when someone is deliberately deceiving you in their communication so you can protect yourself and stay in control of the conversation. Emotional manipulation comes in many forms depending on the individual's personality.

•Passive aggression
This is when the manipulator refuses to voice their issue or negative feelings. Instead of dealing with the problem directly, they find indirect ways to express their anger and undermine or hurt you. Someone who wants to use this on you might agree to take a particular action and then start seeking passive-aggressive ways to let you know they don't want to do it. Instead of saying "no" to your face, they'll fake a "yes." And then they'll procrastinate, become sulky, complain about being underappreciated, exhibit resentment, or ghost you.

• Social and emotional bullying
If you think you can always detect a bully from their non-verbal communication, guess again. Some bullies are professionals at intellectual and bureaucratic bullying. Intellectual bullying is when

someone tries to claim the role of subject matter expert and belittle or demean you when they know you are the pro. Bureaucratic bullying is when someone uses red tape against you to overwhelm or subvert your goals. For example, you walk into a government office. The woman pretends she wants to help you solve your problem. Still, all she does is derail you with paperwork and jargon, all to hide the fact that she remembers you back in high school when you rejected her love poem, and now it's payback.

• Distortion
Sometimes you might be dealing with a personality such as a machiavellian who is pretty intelligent and chooses to manipulate you emotionally by distorting facts or other information needed to assess a situation accurately. They might lie or pretend ignorance about a matter, and they'll do it so naturally that you may not pick it up as a lie. A common but subtle form of this is gaslighting. This is a tactic in which the manipulator causes you to self-doubt, questioning your motivations, abilities, and rights as a human. It happens a lot in the workplace, especially when the boss has manipulative tendencies.

• Guilt and sympathy
Many human beings struggle with feelings of guilt and might even go as far as punishing themselves in response to perceived sins. Emotionally manipulative personalities prey on this human vulnerability. They are apt to play the victim or

constantly remind you of past favors instilling a sense of obligation or sympathy that makes it more likely to cave and give in.

• Withdrawal

Have you ever been in a relationship where your beloved decided to give you the "silent treatment' because of something you did? This is an example of withdrawal. Certain personalities enjoy doing this to others, especially when they're trying to force change or get something they want that the other disagrees with. Sometimes withdrawal happens in more insidious ways. For instance, a wife might withhold sex from her husband as a way of punishing him for doing Friday night football and fun with the boys instead of taking her out for dinner. Whether it's done in the context of intimacy or in the workplace, withholding or withdrawing something from another creates a power imbalance. The person experiencing this will crave that action and seek ways of restoring that usually constitutes meeting the demands of the manipulator.

These are just a handful of ways dark personalities and manipulators distort and attempt to control communication through negative means. It can be challenging to read when someone is manipulating you. Hopefully, the next chapter can give you some tools and tricks to avoid getting caught off guard.

Chapter 07: Non-verbal Cues For Deception

Deception is considered an expression of poor character in our society. No one wants to be associated with a liar, and none of us feel good when accused of lying, but the fact is, we've all lied at some point in our lives. Lies take on all shapes and forms. At times they are tiny omissions of details, and other times they are flat our false information. Observe little children and how easily they lie, and you'll see lying is part of human nature. I mean, no one teaches kids to withhold information or manipulate the truth, yet they do very naturally. When you're attempting to analyze or get a read on someone, the last thing you want is false data that will send you on the wrong path. If someone deliberately communicates falsely, that's exceptionally infuriating and could lead to bigger problems in your relationship. But before we go on an all-out rage fest for discovering that someone just deceived you, let's try to understand the main motives that cause most good-natured people to lie.

Why do people lie?

That might seem like a simple question, but the answer is quite complex. Lying is such a common behavior, and most of us indulge in it for a myriad of reasons. A 2004 Reader's Digest poll found that as many as 96% of people acknowledge that they lie sometimes. But that's not to say we are all pathological liars. One national study published in 2009 that surveyed 1,000 U.S adults found that only about 5% of all the participants were prolific liars.

There are indications that most of us share the same motives for telling lies. If you want to detect lies, you'll need to get better at reading microexpressions but let's not get ahead of ourselves here. First, we need to gain a better understanding of why we lie so much. The Paul Ekman Group did many interviews (children and adults were involved) and collected data that enabled them to give us an expert take on why people lie so much. It turns out, there's a variety of reasons, and the main ones are the following.

• To avoid punishment.
This is the most frequently mentioned motivation for telling lies by both children and adults. According to their surveys, people would lie to avoid punishment whether they were guilty of the accusation or not.

• To obtain a reward they wouldn't otherwise get.
This is the second most frequent motive for deception in both children and adults. An adult will lie about their work experience during a job interview to increase the chances of getting hired.

• To protect a loved one.
Closely connected to the motive of avoiding punishment, people can also lie to protect a loved

one from punishment or harm. We see this often with mothers who lie to the authorities to protect their sons from getting charged for criminal activity. You might also see it in children—for instance, when an older sibling lies to protect a younger one when a mess is made. The same could happen even in the workplace and even with complete strangers, especially when we feel the punishment is unfair.

• For self-defense, especially when one feels like they are in physical danger.
Another reason for lying is when we fear for our lives. For instance, a housewife can pretend she is fine and that her black eye resulted from an attack by a stranger when, in reality, it came from her abusive husband. Because she fears what he would do to her and the kids once they returned home, she would rather protect the secret and give false information.

• To impress others.
Telling lies to win the admiration of others and increase popularity is common among narcissists. It can range from minor white lies told to enhance a story to fabricated personas. Manipulative personalities do it, so naturally, you'd have difficulty picking it up as a lie unless you watch their micro-expressions closely.

• To avoid embarrassment.
Sometimes we tell lies when we really don't want to be embarrassed. It often happens when we are in a new relationship or situation and need to save face.

Children also do it, especially if they feel they've done something their parents would be ashamed of.

• To get out of an awkward social situation.
This is something we've all participated in at some point. If you have a friend or relative who can't stop talking, sometimes the best solution is to pretend another call just came in so you can get out of that conversation. You might also see it play out in the workplace. The ungrateful, demanding boss walks up to you and asks if you're free this weekend, and you say, "gosh no, I have to take my mother to a doctor's appointment, sorry!" The truth is, you just didn't want to work overtime for no pay.

• To maintain privacy.
Usually, this happens when the person has information they don't wish to divulge. So instead, they tell you what you want to hear. For instance, you find out there was a meeting that you weren't invited to, so you ask your colleague what was discussed, and she tells you, "oh, nothing important. Just the upcoming campaign for the new product rollout." She might be lying for many reasons, but perhaps part of it is that the senior leadership just got confirmation that there's a mole in the company, and they're trying to set traps to catch them.

• To manipulate and control others.
This is the most dangerous motive for deception. Dictators like Hilter are famous for doing this. It can be hard to recognize that you're being deceived if the person is also a master communicator because they

have command over their verbal and non-verbal communication. They make sure that you only get the information they want you to have. It takes away your freedom to think, accurately analyze, of making the right decision. Machiavellians and other dark personalities invest a lot of energy, time, and resources to develop this ability.

While other motives might drive people to tell little or big lies that won't neatly fall into any of the above-mentioned categories, I think all lying is rooted in fear. Whether that's a fear of losing control, fear of physical danger, or pain avoidance, deception only occurs when dealing with someone who feels the need to manipulate the situation. And it's not just in politics or business. Lies happen among friends, family, and relatives in our society. The reasons are complicated and often hard to recognize for most lies, especially with a masterful communicator. But there are certain things you can do to tell when you're being lied to.

How to spot a liar

A study found that people could only accurately detect lying 54% of the time in a lab setting. That's hardly impressive. Perhaps the overall difference between lying and honest communication is minuscule, so most people miss it because they don't know how to read in between the lines. You're reading this book, so you can start checking for indicators the average Joe would never think about. Psychologists have utilized research on body language and deception to help members of law enforcement distinguish between truth and lies. Researchers at UCLA conducted studies on the subject. They analyzed 60 studies on deception to develop recommendations and training for law enforcement. These results were published in the American Journal of Forensic Psychiatry. Some of the red flags identified in that report that you should watch out for include:

• The person speaks in sentence fragments (verbal signal).
• Repeating your question each time before answering it.
• Vocal uncertainty. When a person seems unsure or insecure, you will hear it in their tone of voice. Combine that with the act of repeating your question before answering it, and that could be a sign something is off.
• The person will be vague in their response and offer few details. This is a verbal signal whereby the speaker seems to intentionally leave out important details.
• They might play with their hair, press their fingers to their lips, sway their body nervously.
• The person will not provide specific details when you challenge their story. They might also become indifferent, shrugging their shoulders, lacking expression, or attempting to hide their emotions because they don't want you to get to the truth.

If you suspect the person is lying to you, don't rely on body language signals only. While body language cues can hint at deception, research suggests that many expected behaviors are not always associated with lying. Most people assume that eye movements will tell you if someone is lying. Researcher and psychologist Howard Ehrlichman has studied eye movements since the 1970s. Ehrlichman found that eye movements don't signify lying at all. You might think a person is lying because they are shifting their eyes but really, they might be accessing their long-term memory. In short, eye movements are the worst predictors of deception.

The key is to understand which signals to pay attention to and to focus on the right cues. The ones shared are great starting points. You should also listen to your gut because plenty of research points to the fact that most of us have an unconscious, intuitive sense of whether someone is lying or not. Of course, this will require training and the ability to suspend bias and stereotypes when addressing someone.

Chapter 08: The Enneagram Personality Typing

If you're active online, you must have come across a post or two that talks about the Enneagram personality test. It's a popular tool that many people use in the workplace and social settings to learn more about themselves and each other. Although it's quite trendy, this tool is considered to be as ancient as Pythagorean mathematics. Over the years, it has evolved, and various teaches have been modified in different ways to arrive at this modern typing system that we use.

Think of it as a personality typing tool that can break down the patterns of human behavior into specific types, each of which describes the motivations, fears, and strengths of that personality type. For someone who wants to master reading people and their behavior, this is a handy tool to have in your communication tool kit.

Nine personality types are covered in this system that defines a particular core belief about how the world works. When you can understand a person's Enneagram type, you'll quickly start to connect the dots in their behavior. It makes it easier to establish rapport because you'll approach them in a manner they resonate with. The Enneagram can also help you understand how different people react to stress.

It describes how each Enneatype adapts and responds to both stressful and supportive situations. By observing verbal and non-verbal cues, you'll be able to tell what someone is experiencing at that moment.

The Enneagram Symbol

At its simplest form, the Enneagram is a nine-pointed geometric symbol consisting of an outer circle. The nine points (personalities) are numbered clockwise and evenly spaced. There's also a triangle touching points 9, 3, and 6 and an irregular hexagon that connects all the other points, i.e., 1, 2, 4, 5, 7, 8. The circle represents the wholeness or unity of human life, while the other shapes represent how humanity is divided. The types on either side of each core type are called wings. Therefore Enneatype 9 has 8 and 1 as its wings. Enneatype 2 has 1 and 3 as its wings and so on. Many people identify strongly with the description of one or both of their wings, in addition to their primary type. So when you take this test, don't be alarmed to find that you resonate with at least three Enneatypes, two of which will be your wings, and one shall stand as the dominant Enneatype. I usually encourage each individual to take the test themselves and read each Enneatype before using this tool on others. Only through personal experience can the insights in this tool bring more value to your analysis. Many people study the Enneagram and take the tests for their own personal growth and get a deeper insight into their motivations and improve their overall characters.

In addition to understanding your core Enneatype and wings, you might also like to know that there's also an additional connection that you share with two other basic types. For example, suppose you are a type 1. You'll notice two connecting lines, type 7 and type 4. The first line (7) relates to the type you left behind or repressed in childhood. The second line connects to the type you may grow into once you're ready to reach a higher state of development. These connecting lines show how each basic type possesses indispensable strengths. Still, at the same time, we all have darker sides that are full of challenges (the repressed childhood or past). Integrating the past and including all these lines into your development makes you a dynamic individual.

How the Enneagram Works

Let's use you as a case study for this so you can apply this to the people you wish to understand better. Your primary type is largely influenced by biological factors, but it's also impacted by your environmental influences. That includes parental relationships, family dynamics, media influence, etc. The Enneagram assigns a number to your personality type. Since it's a horizontal system of growth, no one number is better than the other. Although experts claim a person can never change from one Enneagram personality to another, they acknowledge that it's possible to resonate with different traits depending on your overall level of health. Speaking of, it's important to note that an Enneatype can have different levels of health, ranging from optimum health to poor health (where negative traits are more pronounced), affecting what personality traits they express.

The Nine Enneagram Type Descriptions

Type 1: The Reformer

The reformer is the rational, idealist type. This person is principled, purposeful, self-controlled, and perfectionistic.

Ones are ethical and conscientious. They have a strong sense of right and wrong and always strive to improve things. Unfortunately, they are often crippled by perfectionism and their fear of making mistakes. Ones are organized, orderly and fastidious, holding themselves to very high standards. It's easy to find them in positions that enable them to fight for a greater good and a better world, such as teaching, crusading, and advocating for change in some way, shape, or form. They can quickly slop into being too critical of themselves, and they typically have problems with resentment and impatience. At their best, they are wise, discerning, realistic, and noble. I like to think of them as morally heroic.

A critical motivation for a type One includes the need to be right. They want to strive higher, improve everything around them, and consistently maintain their ideals. Ones are always looking for self-justifications and moving beyond criticism to not be condemned by anyone.

Basic fear for a type One is the fear of becoming evil or corrupted. They are afraid of being defective. The driving desire for a type One is to be good and to have integrity and balance.

The Enneagram One has the Nine-wing, which is "The Idealist," and the Two-wing, which is "The Advocate." If we look at the two lines of connection for type One, we find it's connected to basic types 4 and 7. That means a type One must become alert to their tendency to become stressed (type 4), which causes them to become moody and irrational, setting them on a path of disintegration. On the positive aspect of things, the connection to type 7 offers growth and integration, and that helps angry, critical type ones to become more joyful and spontaneous like healthy sevens.

Some famous people who have been typed are Nelson Mandela, Prince Charles, Celine Dion, Julie Andrews, Meryl Streep, and Osama bin Laden.

Every Enneatype goes through certain levels of development. Depending on their phase in life, you'll get to interact with that particular expression of their identity when you meet them.

Type One at healthy levels of expression:
Level 1 is when they are at their best. They are extraordinarily wise and discerning. By accepting

what is, they become transcendentally realistic, knowing the best action to take at each moment. Their demeanor is calm, inspiring, and hopeful.

Level 2 is where the person is more conscientious with strong personal convictions. They are keenly aware of right and wrong and greatly value personal religious, and moral values. Their demeanor is rational, reasonable, self-disciplined, and moderate in all things. They do their best to control even their emotions.

Level 3 expresses itself as ethical, truthful, and highly conscientious. Justice and equality really matter to type One at this level. They have a strong sense of responsibility, personal integrity, and a higher purpose. That can make them come across as rigid.

The type One at average levels of expression:
Level 4 dips us into the presence of an average type one who seems dissatisfied with reality and feels the urge to improve everything around them. These are your advocates, crusaders, critics, and so on. They enjoy explaining to others how things "ought to be" and quickly turn into high-minded idealists.

Level 5 is afraid of making mistakes. A type One has ideals to live up to, but fear is very pronounced at this level, which can often cause them to overdo it. They might turn into workaholics in their careers and tend to come across as very rigid and over-controlling. You might associate words like pedantic and fastidious to this particular personality sub-type.

Level 6 is highly critical both of themselves and others. At this level of expression, you'll pick up a lot of perfectionism and judgment. The individual may come across as very picky. Nothing is ever good enough because they always have an opinion of how it should be. This person corrects people around them and works hard to get everyone to do "the right thing" as they see it. Their demeanor is impatient, abrasive, dissatisfied, and at times angry.

Type One at unhealthy levels of expression:

Level 7 is self-righteous, dogmatic, intolerant, and highly judgmental. They feel that they alone know "The Truth," and everyone else is simply wrong. They can be very severe in their actions while finding logical ways to justify them from a moral standpoint.

Level 8 is reasonably unhealthy and tends to obsess about imperfection and wrongdoings (in others, the world, and themselves). Although still aware of their ideals, they struggle to live up to them and often act in opposition to the very truth they preach.

Level 9 is the most unhealthy level for a type to express as they become condemnatory toward others. They tend to experience bouts of depression and nervous breakdowns, and might even attempt suicide. They feel the world is wrong, and truth and justice are missing in the world order, but they don't necessarily feel powerful enough to fix the problems. That makes them cruel and punitive and attracts all kinds of personality disorders and mental health issues.

Type 2: The Helper

The helper is kind, caring, generous, people-pleasing, and possessive. Empathy is the keyword that describes this personality type because they are warm-hearted, friendly, and self-sacrificing. They are well-meaning and driven to seek close connections. Still, they tend to take it too far and enslave themselves just so they can feel needed. At their best, type twos are unselfish and altruistic. They are nurturers and love others unconditionally.

What drives a type two? The need to be loved is at the top of their list. Twos need to be appreciated and acknowledged for their giving. They also care about being heard as they express their feelings. A primary fear they have to contend with is the fear of being unwanted and being unworthy of love.

Enneagram Two has the One-wing, "The Servant," and the Three-wing, "The Host/Hostess." If we look at the two lines of connection for type Two, we find it's connected to basic types 8 and 4. That means type Two must become aware of their tendency to become stressed (type 8), which causes them to become aggressive and dominating, setting them on a path of disintegration. On the positive aspect of things, the connection to type 4 offers growth and integration, and that helps prideful deceptive type twos to become more self-nurturing and emotionally aware.

Some famous people who have been typed as Twos are Eleanor Roosevelt, Lionel Richie, Elizabeth Taylor, Pope John XXIII, Dolly Parton, and Monica Lewinsky.

Type Two at the healthy levels of expression:
Level 1 is when type Two is expressing their highest and best self. At this level of development, the individual is humble, deeply unselfish, and altruistic. They naturally give unconditional love to themselves and others. They carry themselves in a manner that lets you know they live to be in service of others, and they love it.

Level 2 is highly empathetic, compassionate, and cares for others deeply. This person tends to constantly look out for others and care for those around them. They are thoughtful, warm-hearted, forgiving, and sincere. Their demeanor comes across as someone authentic, honest, and easy to read.

Level 3 is expressive, appreciative, and loves to encourage others. They see good in all people. Serving others is very important to them, but they never neglect their own well-being in the name of service. They come across as nurturing, generous, and big-hearted.
Type Two at average levels of expression:

Level 4 is a people-pleaser because they want to be closely connected to others and be seen positively. They come across as overly friendly, emotionally expressive, and perhaps share too much. We know these people always have good intentions, and their heart is in the right place, so we like having them around us even when it gets a bit irritating. Love is what drives them, and they talk about it constantly.

Level 5 is when type Two becomes intrusive and overly intimate. Think of that girlfriend, boyfriend, partner, or spouse who won't give you breathing space. This person needs constant affirmation and reassurance of love and the fact that they are needed. They hover, meddle and control in the name of love (mom, I'm thinking of you). At this level of development, the Twos are only focused on making people dependent on them. Still, they tend to send double messages because it's not always altruistic. Most of the time, they expect that by loving you a lot, you must show them how much you love them back. So they tend to come across as codependent.

Level 6 type Twos can be overbearing, condescending, and presumptuous. They do feel like they give a lot and don't back their fair share, and they also tend to overrate their efforts on others' behalf. A martyr might be a good word to describe how far they are willing to go at this level of development.

Type Two unhealthy levels of expression

Level 7 development sees a turn to the dark side for a type Two. The person becomes manipulative and self-serving, instilling guilt in others and making everyone they helped feel like they owe them. They tend to indulge in self-abuse to get sympathy and attention. Their demeanor is likely inauthentic, deceptive, selfish, and aggressive. They might be in the habit of belittling or undermining people around them.

Level 8 comes with a lot of self-entitlement. At this level, the person feels the world and people owe them, whether material, emotional or otherwise. They become coercive and oppressive.

Level 9 is the unhealthiest level for type Two. At this point, anger, resentment, and bitterness are easy to read from such a person. They tend to feel victimized by the people in their world and assume everyone takes advantage of their good nature. Somatization of their aggressions results in chronic health problems as they vindicate themselves by "falling apart" and burdening others.

Type 03: The Achiever

The achiever is success-oriented, ambitious, adaptable, and energetic.
Success-oriented, charming, and pragmatic are keywords that describe this personality type because they are ever moving toward a goal with zeal and poise. Although they are self-assured and diplomatic, they tend to be concerned with their

public image and what others think of them. At their best, type Threes are perfect role models who inspire others because they come across as authentic and self-accepting.

What drives a type Three? The need for attention and admiration. The type Three individual loves to impress others and wants to be affirmed and seen as unique and different. Type Three desires to feel valuable and worthwhile, which is why they put so much effort into their work and attaining their goals. Competition is something they enjoy and at times take too far. You might also find plenty of type Threes who struggle with workaholism. The greatest fear for a type Three is being worthless.

Enneagram three has the Two-wing, "The Charmer," and the Four-wing, "The Professional." If we look at the two lines of connection for type Three, we find it's connected to basic types 9 and 6. That means a Three must become aware of their tendency to become stressed (type 9), which causes them to become apathetic and disengaged, setting them on a path of disintegration. On the positive aspect of things, the connection to type 6 offers growth and integration, and that helps vain, deceptive Threes become more cooperative and committed to others like healthy Sixes.

Some famous people who have been typed as Threes include Bill Clinton, Muhammed Ali, Oprah Winfrey, Tony Robbins, Deepak Chopra, Tiger Woods, Jon Bon Jovi, Lady Gaga, Tom Cruise, Will

Smith, Cindy Crawford, Anne Hathaway, and Demi Moore.

Type Three at the healthy levels of expression:
Level 1 is when type Three expresses their highest and best self. At this level of development, the individual is self-accepting, authentic, modest, charitable, gentle, and benevolent. Everything they do seems to come from a place of abundance and love.

Level 2 has high self-esteem and self-assurance. This person believes in themselves and their values. They are adaptable, desirable, charming, and gracious in everything they do.

Level 3 is ambitious and focused on self-improvement and self-actualization. This person believes in unlocking their fullest potential. They tend to work hard to embody what they consider ideal human qualities. They tend to attract admiration from others, and people love following this particular type Three.

Type Three at average levels of expression:
Level 4 is highly concerned with performance and doing their job well. There's a constant sense of urgency to achieve goals because their self-worth is tied to achievement. This person tends to be terrified of failure, and they often compare themselves to others. The main driver is status and success in life.

Level 5 is a pragmatic and efficient individual. Still, at this level of development, they may start losing touch with their own feelings and truth. This person is too image-conscious and too concerned with how they are perceived to the point where they might create facades to match that desirable image of success. That's where phoniness comes into play. You'll notice the person struggling with intimacy and credibility because they are willing to do anything to be perceived as the best.

Level 6 type Threes want to impress others by appearing superior. This person constantly promotes themselves and wants everyone around them to perceive them as "best in class," even when it's false. They tend to exhibit narcissistic qualities and can come across as highly arrogant. Jealousy is a common emotion at this level of development because the person feels other people shouldn't be further ahead or more successful.

Type Three unhealthy levels of expression
Level 7 development sees a turn to the dark side for a type Three. Fear of failure and humiliation are big issues at this level. This person builds on the illusion of success and superiority, assuming that they can get away with fooling others. They tend to be opportunistic, exploitative, and jealous of the success of others and aren't afraid to cross lines to preserve their illusion.

Level 8 comes with a lot of deception and self-centeredness. At this level, the person is delusionally jealous of others, feeling that they deserve the success others enjoy. They become malicious and devious, often betraying or sabotaging people to grab what they believe is rightfully theirs.

Level 9 is the unhealthiest level for type Three. At this point, they become obsessive about destroying whatever reminds them of their shortcomings and failures. Typically the individual will be vindictive and exhibit psychopathic behaviors. Many are diagnosed with some form of Narcissistic Personality Disorder.

Type 4: The Individualist

The individualist is honest, creative, sensitive, and highly self-aware.
Creativity is the keyword that describes this personality type because they seek new ways to be inspired and express their creativity. They are also very sensitive, emotional, and introspective, making them extremely moody and withdrawn. At their best, type Fours are inspired and highly creative. They can renew themselves and transform even the most mundane into something magical.

What drives a type Four? The need to self-express and self-actualize, ultimately creating their self-identity. Nothing is more important to a Four than being able to express their individuality. A primary fear they have to contend with is the fear of lacking identity or personal significance.

Enneagram Four has the Three-wing, "The Aristocrat," and the Five-wing, "The Bohemian." If we look at the two lines of connection for type Four, we find it's connected to basic types 2 and 1. That means a type Four must become aware of their tendency to become stressed (type 2), which causes them to become too clingy and self-involved, setting them on a path of disintegration. On the positive aspect of things, the connection to type 1 offers growth and integration, which helps envious and emotionally turbulent Fours become more objective and principles like healthy Ones.

Some famous people who have been typed as Fours include Angelina Jolie, Winona Ryder, Jonny Depp, Virginia Woolf, Rumi, Cher, Prince, Alanis Morrisette, and Nicolas Cage.

Type Four at the healthy levels of expression:
Level 1 is when type Four expresses their best and highest self. At this level of development, the Four is profoundly creative, expressing the personal and universal (mainly in the form of art). They are inspired, self-renewing, regenerating, and every experience is valuable, transformative, and magical.

Level 2 is highly self-aware and reflective. The Four is searching for the "self" and spends all their time embarking on activities that facilitate this quest. They are sensitive and intuitive to both themselves and others. Character-wise they come across as gentle, tactful, and compassionate.

Level 3 is highly individualistic and "true to self" only. They are emotionally honest and humane. Although still attempting to understand self and solidify their identity, they are emotionally strong, funny yet serious, and have no problem being vulnerable.

Type Four at average levels of expression:
Level 4 is obsessed with beauty, romance, and art in life. This individual loves to create a beautiful aesthetic environment to cultivate and prolong personal feelings. A Four at this level experiences heightened reality through fantasy and spends a lot of time in the imagination.

Level 5 is when type Four begins to introspect too much. They tend to become self-absorbed and take everything personally. A Four at this level is moody, hypersensitive, and often introverted. They are unable to "get out of themselves" and tend to be. Withdrawn from society to protect their self-image and buy time to sort out their emotions.

Level 6 type Four can be increasingly impractical and unproductive as they fall out of touch with their feelings. They tend to become melancholy dreamers, disdainful, decadent and sensual, living in a fantasy world. Some drown in self-pity, feeling like they are different from others and can't live as everyone else does.

Type Four unhealthy levels of expression

Level 7 development sees a turn to the dark side for a type Four. The person becomes ashamed of self and likely struggles with bouts of depression. At this point, many of the individual's dreams don't come to fruition, and they turn resentful and angry for their self failure. They will alienate themselves from others because they don't want to deal with reality as is. Their demeanor is likely resentful, exhausted, and has emotional paralysis. It's tough to reason with a Four at this level.

Level 8 comes with a lot of self-loathing and contempt. At this level, the person likes to blame others for their torment. The world has lost all its beauty, and everything is a source of suffering. This Four is highly cynical and pessimistic toward themselves and everyone else. Usually, they don't want anyone getting close and drive away any kind of support.

Level 9 is the unhealthiest level for a type Four. At this point, hopelessness, powerlessness, and despair are what you read from such a person. They cannot be trusted to make sound judgments even with their own lives and tend to become hazardous to themselves and the world. It's very common for a Four at this level to have suicidal thoughts and even get away with it. When a highly creative, emotional, and imaginative person goes totally dark, they usually attempt to soothe that torment with alcohol, drugs, and other addictive substances.

Anger, resentment, and bitterness are easy to read from such a person. You'll notice this person is avoidant and mentally unstable.

Type 5: The Investigator

The investigator is intense, alert, insightful, perceptive, innovative, focused, and inventive. Independence is the keyword that describes this personality type because they most enjoy being on their own. They are very secretive and detached from the connections many of us want. Fives enjoy developing complex ideas and skills and using their thoughts, imagination, and time to create new and better solutions.

At their best, type Fives are visionary pioneers and usually ahead of their time. They can see what others can't, and they enjoy reimagining the world in new unconventional ways.

What drives a type Five? They need to gain knowledge, understand their environment and figure things out. Nothing is more important to a Five than feeling capable enough to defend themselves from the environmental threats they perceive. A primary fear they have to contend with is feeling incapable, helpless, or being useless.

Enneagram Five has the Four-wing, which is "The Iconoclast," and the Six-wing, which is "The Problem Solver." If we look at the two lines of connection for a type Five, we find it's connected to basic types 7 and 8. That means a Five must become aware of their tendency to become stressed (type 7), which causes them to become dangerously detached and scattered, setting them on a path of disintegration. On the positive aspect of things, the connection to type 8 offers growth and integration, and that helps detached Fives become more self-confident and decisive like healthy Eights.

Some famous people who have been typed as Fives include Albert Einstein, Stephen Hawkin, Bill Gates, Jane Goodall, Jodie Foster, and Eckhart Tolle.

Type Five at the healthy levels of expression:
Level 1 is when type Five expresses their best and highest self. At this level of development, the Five is open-minded and visionary in all they do. They are capable of making discoveries and pioneering ideas that take things to a whole new level. Their demeanor is often a high level of confidence and perceptiveness. They have a certain intensity in their eye that's awe-inspiring. This Five is known for doing and perceiving things in ways the ordinary person cannot comprehend.

Level 2 is mentally alert and curious. They observe everything with extraordinary perceptiveness and insight. Their ability to concentrate is off the charts, and they possess great foresight and prediction. Nothing intelligent and valuable escapes their notices, especially once they decide what to go after. This Five tends to come across as profoundly intense and almost obsessive.

Level 3 is ever excited by knowledge. Once they set their eyes on a topic or skill, they will wholeheartedly pursue it and become the expert in their field. They are very knowledgeable and great at producing precious, original works. Their demeanor comes across as whimsical and highly independent.

Type Five at average levels of expression:
Level 4 is more of intellect and tends to challenge the current status quo of things when working on a project. This Five spends a lot of time working things out in their mind and building mental models. Research, preparation, and practice are essential to a five at this level because they enjoy conceptualizing and fine-tuning everything before taking any action.

Level 5 is when a type Five begins to detach a bit more from reality. They become too preoccupied with their visions and interpretations of their complex ideas. A Five at this level is high strung and intense, often fascinated by off-beat, esoteric subjects, including those that involve dark elements.

Level 6 type Five take an antagonistic stance toward anything that interferes with their inner world and personal vision. They become cynical and argumentative. You might notice this person's views are radical and abrasive.

Type Five unhealthy levels of expression

Level 7 development sees a turn to the dark side for a type Five. The person becomes a recluse isolating themselves from anything that doesn't align with their personal vision, including reality. At this point, you'll observe mental instability and fear, and they are not interested in any social attachments.

Level 8 is where a Five becomes negatively obsessive and frightened by their ideas, becoming horrified and delirious. At this point, you'll notice the person struggles with phobias and gross distortions, which negatively impact how they function in life.

Level 9 is the unhealthiest level for a type Five. At this point, that intensity and obsessive behavior are so consumed by the darkness that suicide or a psychotic breakdown is likely to happen. This Five is deranged, self-destructive and generally correspond to the Schizoid Avoidant and Schizotypal personality disorders.

Type 6: The Loyalist

The loyalist is committed, trustworthy, hard-working, reliable, and excellent at solving problems. Responsibility is the keyword that describes this personality type because they take their commitments very seriously. They are excellent troubleshooters and enjoy fostering collaborations and helping people unlock their fullest potential. They like feeling secure and creating a sense of stability and security for the people around them.
At their best, type Sixes are emotionally stable, self-reliant, courageous, and passionate about championing themselves and others.

What drives a type Six? The need to be secure, to support, and be supported by others. Sixes need reassurance and certainty, which can sometimes be challenging in a world that is constantly changing. Nothing is more important to a Six than having a strong support system and creating structures that help them feel grounded and protected.

A primary fear they have to contend with is the fear of being abandoned, lacking support and guidance.

Enneagram Six has the Five-wing, "The Defender," and the Seven-wing, "The Buddy." If we look at the two lines of connection for a type Six, we find it's connected to basic types 3 and 9. That means a Six must become aware of their tendency to become stressed (type 3), which causes them to become overly competitive and arrogant, setting them on a path of disintegration. On the positive aspect of things, the connection to type 9 offers growth and integration, and that helps pessimistic and anxious Sixes become more relaxed and optimistic like healthy Nines.

Some famous people who have been typed as Sixes include Sigmund Freud, Mark Twain, Diana Princess of Wales, U2's Bono, Mike Tyson, Sally Field, Tom Hanks, Julia Roberts, Jennifer Aniston, Ben Affleck, Ellen Degeneres, and Chris Rock.

Type Six at the healthy levels of expression:
Level 1 is when type Six is expressing their best and highest self. At this level of development, the Six is

self-affirming, confident, trusting of self and others. The person comes across as independent, grounded, and yet symbolically interdependent. They cooperate with others and treat them as equals. Character-wise they are optimistic, courageous, loyal, and rich in self-expression. They also have a natural tendency to lead others wholeheartedly.

Level 2 is very appealing, lovable, and affectionate with others. Trust is vital to this Six, especially when forming relationship bonds and alliances. In observation, you will pick this up in the words they use and the ideas they share.

Level 3 is dedicated to individuals and standing up for causes they believe in. They are "loyal" to the cause, as is often said. This Six is a community builder and comes across as very hard-working, trustworthy, reliable, and always there for you. They can persevere almost anything and are willing to sacrifice for others. In observation, you'll notice that this is the kind of person who brings a cooperative spirit into everything and likes to create a sense of stability and security in every setting.

Type Six at average levels of expression:
Level 4 is more focused on things that make them feel safe and stable. At this point, the Six is already starting to experience anxiety about everything they can't control. They invest a lot of time organizing and structuring, finding alliances and authoritative figures that offer security and continuity. Their demeanor comes across as vigilant and a bit anxious.

Level 5 is when a Six starts to become indecisive, cautious, and evasive. At this point, they tend to procrastinate on things as they resist having more demands made of them. Their outlook is ambivalent and can become quite reactive to situations. In observation, this person will send you all kinds of mixed signals, making them a bit unpredictable. Passive aggression is often their go-to communication style. They can contradict themselves quite a bit, saying one thing and doing the opposite.

Level 6 is where a type Six begins to feel their insecurities mounting. They might become very sarcastic ad belligerent. At this level, the six dishes out a lot of blame and becomes highly reactive and defensive. This person sees the world in black and white; friends and enemies, and they are highly suspicious of everything and everyone. They are highly concerned with conspiracy theories and self-conservation because threats are becoming more and more unmanageable.

Type Six unhealthy levels of expression

Level 7 development sees a turn to the dark side for a type Six. That's where a Six becomes volatile, panic-stricken, and self-disparaging. Feelings of inferiority start to run their mind, and they see themselves as defenseless. Typically, a six at this level will seek a stronger authority figure or belief to resolve all problems. In observation, you can pick up their inferiority complex and fears through the words they use, their highly divisive attitude, and how easily they criticize others.

Level 8 is where a Six starts lashing out and acting irrationally. In effect, they self manufacture the very things they fear. At this point, the six feels persecuted and threatened by an external and often invisible (only real to their mind) "them." That can often turn them into violent individuals.

Level 9 is the unhealthiest level for a type Six, and at this point, you'll pick up on a lot of clues that signal the person is not well. Alcoholism, drug abuse, and other self-abusing behavior are apparent with this Six. They might also exhibit passive-aggressive behavior and paranoia, causing them to be quite hysterical. Often the person seeks to escape from the punishment that threatens their life. In extreme cases, these individuals are highly self-destructive and should be handled with care.

Type 7: The Enthusiast

The enthusiast is optimistic, spontaneous, playful, and versatile.
Playfulness and adventure are the keywords that describe this personality type because they seek exciting new experiences. They get bored quickly and don't like being confined by rules or discipline. Although they are very practical and highly talented, they tend to over-extend themselves, making it difficult to reach one specific goal excellently.

At their best, type Sevens are focused on pursuing worthwhile goals and leveraging their talents. They are joyous, satisfied, fun to be around, and highly stimulating.

What drives a type Seven? The longing for freedom and happiness. They desire to have their needs fulfilled and to experience satisfaction in life. They also need to experience as much as possible because they hate missing out on fun and exciting things. A basic fear they have to contend with is the fear of missing out, lacking something in life, and experiencing pain. Nothing is more important to a Seven than pain avoidance.

Enneagram Seven has the Six-wing, which is "The Entertainer," and the Eight-wing, which is "The Realist." If we look at the two lines of connection for a type Seven, we find it's connected to basic types 1 and 5. That means a Seven must become aware of their tendency to become stressed (type 1), which causes them to become perfectionistic and critical of everything setting them on a path of disintegration. On the positive aspect of things, the connection to type 8 offers growth and integration, and that helps gluttonous, scattered Sevens become more focused and fascinated by life, just like healthy Fives.

Some famous people who have been typed as Sevens include The 14th Dalai Lama, W.A. Mozart, Amelia Earhart, Ram Dass, Richard Branson, Elton John, Katy Perry, Robin Williams, Jim Carrey, Robert

Downey, Jr., Leonardo DiCaprio, Charlie Sheen, Paris Hilton, Cary Grant, and Bette Midler.

Type Sevens at the healthy levels of expression:
Level 1 is when type Seven expresses their best and highest self. At this level of development, the Seven is awed by the simple wonders of life. They are joyous and ecstatic. They are spiritual and embrace the boundless goodness of life. This Seven assimilates experiences in-depth, making the person profoundly grateful and appreciative for what they have. Being around them is simply invigorating because they radiate such great energy. They've learned to focus their energy and talent positively, which makes them highly productive.

Level 2 is highly responsive, excitable, enthusiastic about sensation and experience. Most people at this level are extroverted in personality type, and they seek anything and everything to stimulate their senses. In character, these people are cheerful, spontaneous, vivacious, lively, and exceptionally resilient. They seem to bounce back very fast from any setbacks or challenges.

Level 3 is practical, productive, and usually multi-talented. They are great at accomplishing their goals and tend to do many things exceptionally well-cross-fertilizing areas of interest. They are prolific thinkers and tend to be great conversationalists.

Type Seven at average levels of expression:
Level 4 is restless and needs to have more options and choices than the other healthy Sevens. This Seven needs more variety and is constantly seeking new external things to satiate their thirst for more. As a consumer, these Sevens are big spenders, and they need more money, more variety s they can keep up with trends.

Level 5 is when a type Seven becomes hyperactive and unable to control their thirst for more. At this point, they struggle to discern what they really need in life, so they throw themselves into constant activity. Ever busy and occupied with things to avoid being bored, they tend to fall into extreme situations and exaggerated performances. While they still have plenty of ideas and lots of talents, there's very little follow-through or complete execution.

Level 6 type Seven takes a turn into excess consumption. This Seven is materialistic, greedy, too self-focused, and never feel like they have enough. At this point, the person becomes pushy, insensitive, jaded, and quickly falls into addictive behavior.

Type Seven unhealthy levels of expression

Level 7 development sees a turn to the dark side for a type Seven. The person becomes desperate to quell their anxieties, making them infantile and impulsive. In other words, this Seven doesn't know when to stop. They can't control their behaviors, so they fall into addiction. Often you'll observe them as abusive, offensive, and depraved.

Level 8 is where a Seven begins to project the inner torment and restlessness onto others. In an attempt to run from the self that is now out of control, this Seven will become erratic, moody, and compulsive in their behavior.

Level 9 is the unhealthiest level for a type Seven. At this point, all that hunger for adventure and energy is completely drained. They become claustrophobic and panic-stricken. This Seven tend to give up on themselves and life. They become depressive, self-destructive and it's not uncommon for them to contemplate suicide. Many Sevens who land into addiction tend to end up overdosing once they hit this rock bottom.

Type 8: The Challenger

The challenger is self-confident, assertive, resourceful, decisive, and strong. Powerful and in control are the keywords that describe this personality type. However, sometimes that can come off as being intimidating and overpowering. Eights are straight-talkers, and they are not afraid of confrontations. They are very protective of those they feel responsible for and will go to great lengths to provide and "lead the herd." At their best, type Eights are heroic, strong, magnanimous, and care a lot about self-mastery. That makes them highly inspiring and natural-born leaders. People feel safe and willingly follow an Eight who has unlocked their potential.

What drives a type Eight? They need to be self-reliant and protect themselves and those they care about. Nothing is more important to an Eight than proving that they are strong and in control of things. Eights want to be important in the world and to build a legacy. A basic fear they have to contend with is the fear of being controlled by others or losing their power somehow.

Enneagram Eight has the Seven-wing, "The Maverick," and the Nine-wing, "The Bear." If we look at the two lines of connection for a type Eight, we find it's connected to basic types 2 and 5. That means an Eight must become aware of their tendency to become stressed (type 5), which causes them to become secretive and fearful, setting them on a path of disintegration. On the positive aspect of things, the connection to type 2 offers growth and integration, and that helps lustful Eights become more open-hearted and caring like healthy Twos.

Some famous people who have been typed as Eights include Fidel Castro, Donald Trump, Sean Connery, James Brown, Frank Sinatra, Fidel Castro, Serena Williams, Clint Eastwood, Sean Penn, Alec Baldwin, Pablo Picasso, and Ernest Hemingway.

Type Eight at the healthy levels of expression:
Level 1 is when type Eight is expressing their best and highest self. At this level of development, the

Eight is magnanimous, self-controlled, merciful, and forbearing. They possess a lot of courage and self-surrender and may achieve historical greatness and real heroism. At this level of development, and Eight will gladly put themselves in serious jeopardy to achieve their vision and have a lasting influence.

Level 2 is self-assertive, confident, and strong. This Eight knows how to stand up for themself. They are usually very resourceful, always getting what they need and want. Their demeanor is very appealing, with lots of passion, inner drive, and a "can-do" attitude that attracts everyone into their world.

Level 3 is protective, honorable, and often champions people. This Eight isn't afraid to take the initiative and commandeer others to victory. In observation, you will find this person decisive, sharp, strong, and a natural-born leader who loves to be the provider.

Type Eight at average levels of expression:
Level 4 is more concerned about having enough resources. This Eight will focus more on attaining financial independence and being self-sufficient. They take great risks, work hard, and are very pragmatic. Unfortunately, at this point, the person neglects their emotional needs and tries very hard to suppress and deny emotions.

Level 5 is when a type Eight begins to lean more towards domination. They want to dominate and control their environment and others. In demeanor, they will come across as boastful, forceful, egocentric, and proud. This Eight wants to be seen as the "boss" whose word is the law. At this level of development, the person struggles with equality and wants to impose themselves and their ideas on everyone.

Level 6 type Eight takes on the insecure path, becoming more off-balanced and egocentric. This Eight is highly combative, intimidating, and has a terrible temper. You'll observe a lot of confrontation, issuing of threats, and unjust treatment to force obedience and respect.

Type Eight unhealthy levels of expression

Level 7 development sees a turn to the dark side for a type Eight, and it is ugly. The person becomes completely ruthless, dictatorial, and potentially violent. This Eight is hard-hearted and fights anyone who tries to reason with or control them.

Level 8 is where an Eight becomes delusional about their power, invincibility, and invulnerability. Somehow they convince themselves that they are omnipotent and untouchable. At this point, they become reckless and over-extend themselves.

Level 9 is the unhealthiest level for a type Eight. At this point, the person is not only vengeful, but they are also extremely dangerous. Anything that threatens their survival is ruthlessly destroyed, and they often develop sociopathic tendencies.

Type 9: The Peacemaker

The peacemaker is easy-going, trusting, accepting, optimistic and supportive. Peaceful is the keyword that describes this personality type because they most enjoy creating harmony and stability around them at any cost. Sometimes they will go along with something just to keep the peace. At their best, type Nines are healers. They are all-embracing and can bring people together and create a sense of safety and unity around them.

What drives a type Nine? The need to maintain inner and outer peace. They love to preserve things as they are and maintain inner peace of mind and stability. Nothing is more important to a Nine than creating harmony in their environment. A basic fear they have to contend with is fear of loss and separation.

Enneagram Nine has the Eight-wing, which is "The Referee," and the One-wing, which is "The Dreamer." If we look at the two lines of connection for a type Nine, we find it's connected to basic types 3 and 6. That means a Nine must become aware of their tendency to become stressed (type 6), which causes them to become complacent, anxious, and worried, setting them on a path of disintegration. On the positive aspect of things, the connection to type 3 offers growth and integration, and that helps slothful Nines become more energetic and self-developing like healthy Threes.

Some famous people who have been typed as Nines include Queen Elizabeth II, Abraham Lincoln, Carl Jung, Walt Disney, George Lucas, Janet Jackson, Lisa Kudrow, Morgan Freeman, Kevin Costner, and Whoopie Goldberg.

Type Nine at the healthy levels of expression:
Level 1 is when type Nine expresses their best and highest self. At this level of development, the Nine is creative, autonomous, self-controlled, and fulfilled in every way possible. They have great equanimity and contentment because they are present to themselves. This Nine can be at one with self and with others; therefore, they have profoundly deep and nourishing relationships. Often you will find that Nines at this level can heal people, situations, and environments either knowingly or unknowingly. People are simply drawn to the presence of this Nine, and their demeanor is a sense of aliveness and connectedness that is truly extraordinary.

Level 2 is deeply receptive, self-accepting, emotionally stable, and serene. They trust themselves and others. This Eight is at ease with life, patient with others, unpretentious, good-natured, and genuinely nice. People are highly drawn to this Nine.

Level 3 is ever reassuring and supportive with others. They have a calming and healing influence and are great at harmonizing groups. This nine enjoys bringing people together and often becomes a great mediator, synthesizer, and communicator.

Type Nine at average levels of expression:
Level 4 often idealizes others and "goes along" with other people's wishes even when they don't really want to. This Nine feels the need to accommodate everyone and often falls into conventional roles and expectations.

Level 5 is when a type Nine becomes indifferent in life. They might be active in society and at work, but they are disengaged, unreflective and inattentive. This Nine has made a decision that they don't want to be affected by problems or face harsh realities, so they "tune out."

Level 6 type Nine is stubborn, fatalistic, and resigned as if nothing could be done to change anything. This Nine typically falls into wishful thinking and magical solutions, and they also become massive procrastinators.

Type Nine unhealthy levels of expression

Level 7 development sees a turn to the dark side for a type Nine. The person becomes neglectful, repressed, and ineffectual. This Nine feels incapable of facing any problem causing them to become obstinate.

Level 8 is where a Nine makes themselves numb and depersonalized in an attempt to block out any awareness of problems they feel helpless to solve.

Level 9 is the unhealthiest level for a type Nine. At this point, the person is severely disoriented and catatonic, abandoning themselves and turning into shattered shells. Looking into their eyes, all you see is a hollow figure of a person in complete resignation and utter despair.

Section Three: Emotional Intelligence Quotient

Chapter 09: Introduction To Emotional Intelligence

Dan Goleman popularized this term "emotional intelligence," aka EI aka EQ, in his 1996 book titled Emotional Intelligence. Although the term was coined by two researchers (Peter Salovey and John Mayer) back in 1990, it recently got a spotlight in social and professional settings. Today, you'll hear statements such as "a great leader must have high emotional intelligence" or "EI is more important than IQ if you want to succeed in life." But what exactly is emotional intelligence? Goleman defines it as the ability to recognize, understand and manage our own emotions and also to recognize, understand and influence the feelings of others. From a practical standpoint, having a high EI is very advantageous to a masterful communicator. One might argue that it is the key to effective communication and influence.

That means you must be aware of the emotions that drive your behavior and how that impacts people (positively or negatively) and at the same time learn how you can manage those emotions - both yours and other people's. Managing emotions is especially important in situations where you're communicating under pressure. If you need to quickly analyze someone whole in a job interview, a boardroom meeting with your shareholders, giving and receiving feedback, or even with a beloved, you need the ability to intuit where the conversation is going so you can steer it the right way.

How badly do you want to succeed?

At a personal level, emotional intelligence will help you have uncomfortable conversations without hurtful feelings. You'll improve your relationships and have an easier time reading between the lines when people communicate with you. At work, you'll efficiently resolve conflicts and build psychological safety when people interact with you.

EQ versus IQ

A Harvard Business School research determined that EQ counts for twice as much as IQ and technical skills combined to determine an individual's success. A 2003 Harvard Business Review reported that 80% of competencies that differentiate top performers from others are in the domain of Emotional Intelligence. In other words, the thing that makes a person most productive and effective and separates them from the rest of the pack is EI. We could make the same argument on the ability to read people effectively. You can read all the books you want on speed reading, learn tricks, tools, and techniques for speed reading. Still, if you don't increase your Emotional Intelligence Quotient, you won't be as effective at accurately determining what an individual conveys with their non-verbal signals. The good news is that almost anyone can cultivate emotional intelligence.

How to cultivate your EI

Without realizing it, we naturally gravitate toward a person with a high EQ. This individual tends to put everyone at ease, and it feels like they "get us." Have you ever met someone like that? Well, now I want you to become such an individual. When you can make people feel safe around you, they will open up and reveal their true selves effortlessly. After all, who doesn't want a boss, friend, parent, colleague, or businessman who understands what they are feeling and what they care about?
To become this man, you need first to learn how to identify the emotions you're experiencing. You also need to understand and accept them.

Men struggle with this part because it doesn't seem to be a manly thing to discuss emotions. Haven't we been encouraged to be unemotional and 100% rational? Isn't that what makes a real man?
It turns out that's one of the big lies going around. Real alpha men aren't controlled, calm, and cool because their emotions are suppressed. Instead, they are relaxed and self-controlled because they are aware and in tune with their feelings. They have learned to keep their emotions in check in a healthy way. Read that last paragraph several times until it sinks in. Here is a step-by-step process you can take to improve your EI and, ultimately, get a bearing on other people's emotions.

Step one. Observe how you react around people.
The first and most important step in cultivating higher EI is to increase self-awareness. Become more aware of your emotions by monitoring yourself throughout the day. You can set a timer where you pause for a minute and do a self-check. Notice how you feel and what events transpired to trigger those feelings. Practicing mindfulness will also enable you to tune in to your emotions. Once you acknowledge the emotion and examine the environmental and triggers that led to that emotion, decide to act in accordance with your character. This is how you start ruling over your emotions instead of suppressing them or, worse, still denying them.

Step two. Seek to understand the points of view of others.
Once you better understand how you feel, react, and deal with different situations and environments, it's time to shift focus. Start noticing the points of view and emotions of those around you. To do this, listen attentively and become aware of the non-verbal cues people send off in different situations. Have you seen some of those movements before? Perhaps you've carried yourself in the same manner? The investigator in you who gathered data on your emotions and behavior will play a huge role in assisting you in deciphering what others are trying to convey. It would help if you also started creating buffer periods as you communicate with others. That way, you can put yourself in their shoes briefly to see what could cause them to behave or speak as they do.

By stretching your perspective and awareness in this way, you get a better reading of the other person.

Step three. Pay close attention to their non-verbal communication and engage your active listening skills.

Step four. Show the other person that you are interested and that you care. Be genuinely invested in that conversation, and you will establish a connection. Whether you are an introvert or an extrovert, you can develop fast connections with others.

Active listening, open body language posture, and facial expressions are just some of the ways you can show the other person that you are present and interested in what they are communicating.

Step five. Practice some emotional management. Tune into your emotions at that particular time and those of the person you're interacting with. Stop and take time to process and understand what is transpiring. If you feel your emotions flare up or things start getting heated, divert your attention until you become more composed, e.g., step away from that room or ask for a short break and go for a brisk walk. By giving yourself some room to breathe, you can bring your emotions back to balance and keep them in check. Another approach is to mentally step back and look at the big picture to determine how vital that immediate emotional reaction is to the overall issue. This hack is used by almost every powerful and calm leader you know. They don't lack emotions (at least not the good ones), but rather, they know how to quickly breathe and zoom out, so the main agenda remains a priority instead of their immediate impulse to cause a fit.

As you can see, cultivating emotional intelligence isn't rocket science, but it does take time and practice. Start with these five steps and then move to advanced training and technique for best results. Ultimately, you want to understand yourself and others better by tapping into the realm of emotions. Gain mastery over your feelings, and you'll have the natural ability to predict and decipher the emotions that others leak out as they communicate.

Chapter 10: Different Emotions And Different Signals

Imagine if I told you that with just one look at a "special map," you'd have the power to know something very personal about other people - their feelings! Would that thrill you? For most men, this would be like finding the holy grail (especially married men). Knowing whether someone is bored, sad, angry, or happy could save you a lot of time and energy. The whole purpose of this book is to help you become a better communicator. That means you learn to express yourself better, and more importantly, you know to read what others are telling. That way, you can be more in control of the situation. It's easier to control a situation when the person speaks genuinely, but what about when you're dealing with an emotional person?

Most men struggle to understand or identify what others are feeling at any given moment because they haven't yet activated the superpower that reads the unique map commonly known as "the human face."

I say it's a superpower because, for most guys, reading microexpressions doesn't come easy. To get better and faster at decoding non-verbal communication, learn to master reading emotions through facial expressions because they almost always tell the truth behind that person's words. Dr. Paul Ekman says that there are 7 "universal" emotions that every human on the planet makes when they feel intense emotion. Since we are always drawn to look at the face when interacting with others, picking up a person's dominant emotions can quickly help you figure out their state of mind and intentions. In this chapter, we'll look at how people use and interpret these emotions in everyday life.

The basic theory of emotions

Many theories and schools of thought focus on the study and understanding of emotions, but we will focus on the theory developed by Paul Ekman (UWA Online, 2019). Ekman's theory suggests that some feelings are universal and can be identified through certain facial expressions, discussed shortly. These emotions are anger, happiness, sadness, surprise, contempt, disgust, and fear. Another theory was put forth by psychologist Robert Plutchik known as the "wheel of emotions," It works similar to a color wheel. According to this theory, more basic emotions act like building blocks to form different feelings, much like colors can be mixed to create other shades. For example, basic emotions such as happiness/joy and trust can be combined to create love.

In recent years, this research has evolved even further, confirming the existence of far more basic emotions than previously believed, raising the number to 27 different categories of emotion. There are also a variety of universal facial expressions, and ongoing studies show that we may share at least sixteen complex expressions. Amusement, anger, awe, concentration, confusion, contempt, contentment, desire, disappointment, doubt, elation, interest, pain, sadness, surprise, and triumph. The trick to awakening your superpower and quickly reading these expressions when others make it is to practice making the facial expressions that go along with these sixteen emotions in front of a mirror.

A deeper look at microexpressions:

Microexpressions are minor and very temporary expressions that you can read on someone's face if you're a keen observer. These come and go in less than half a second, but they are the secret to having superhuman abilities to read people's emotions. Microexpressions are often connected with deeper feelings that a person is usually trying to conceal. Think of it like a leak that someone is trying to cover up. Ever heard of the term "read between the line"? Microexpressions will turn you into a master of this technique. When you can read someone's microexpressions, you can tell whether they are truthful, genuine, or deceptive with their information. Spotting and analyzing micro-expressions is tough, but it's a skill that will grow stronger with practice. Before we discuss how to identify and read microexpressions, let's unpack the main universal emotions.

Emotions and their interpretations

Happiness

Our society tends to be driven by the need to experience more happiness, and it seems to be the most sought-after emotion. Happiness has different definitions, but let's agree that it is a pleasant emotional state characterized by feelings of joy, satisfaction, contentment, and well-being at its most basic form. There's plenty of research on happiness, with several disciplines coming up since the 1960s, including positive psychology. There are even online courses that teach you how to be happy. But how can you tell when someone is genuinely conveying happiness?

To start with, their tone of voice will be upbeat, pleasant, and enthusiastic. Their body language will be relaxed with an open posture, and a genuine smile will form on their face. As the eyebrows are slightly raised, the eyelids will wrinkle up and form "crow's feet." Watch for cue clusters such as arms and legs uncrossed, eyes twinkling, laugh lines on the corner of the eyes, raised cheeks, and exposed teeth.

Microexpressions for happiness
No one can fake real happiness even though people try to do it all the time to no avail. When someone is truly happy, you'll observe what's known as a Duchenne smile. What's a Duchenne smile? Coined by French neurologist Guillaume Duchenne, this is the kind of smile that comes from true enjoyment

and can be distinguished from a fake smile by the *orbicularis oculi* muscle, which forms crow's feet wrinkles around the eyes. You'll also notice the lips are drawn back and up. The mouth may or may not be parted and teeth exposed.

Surprise

Surprise is usually brief and characterized by a psychological startle response following something unexpected. Although we associate surprise with positive emotions, it can also elicit negative (shocking) or neutral emotions. An example of a positive and pleasant feeling is when you arrive home after a long day working late into the night to find your wife awake waiting for you with a warm bath and your favorite childhood comfort meal made from scratch. I think any husband would immediately feel a pleasant feeling from such a loving act instead of the usual foul look for missing date night again.

An unpleasant surprise might be someone jumping out from behind the dumpster and scaring you as you walk to your car at night. Shock is often characterized by verbal reactions such as gasping, screaming, or yelling. You might also notice a physical response whereby the person jumps back because they didn't see or hear you enter the room. Typically with the face, you'll notice eyebrows raising, eyes widening, and mouth opening. Depending on the kind of surprise we're dishing out, the person on the receiving end may experience a burst of adrenaline that could trigger the fight or flee response, so be mindful of how you surprise someone.

Microexpressions of surprise
The microexpressions of surprise are easy enough to spot. Simply pay attention to the eye area and the mouth. The eyebrows will raise and curve, stretching the skin below the brow. Horizontal wrinkles will show across the forehead, and the eyelids will be wide open. So wide that you can actually see the white of the eye above and below. The jaw drops open, and the teeth are parted, but there won't be any tension or stretching of the mouth.

Fear

Fear is one of the most powerful, primitive, and naturally occurring human emotions that seems to be wired in all of us. It involves a universal biochemical response as well as a high individual emotional response. Fear lets us know that we are in the presence of danger or something that threatens our safety and survival. Sometimes the fear stems from real threats, but other times it comes from imagined dangers. If the person you're interacting with experiences some sort of fear, they immediately go through what's known as the fight or flight response. You'll observe a cluster of cues, including increased breathing rate, rapid eye blinking, increased heart rate, muscle tension, and they will take on a stance that helps them either hide, flee or fight whatever is threatening them. Of course, different people react differently to fear. Some people might start trembling, crying, or experience a dry throat.

Microexpressions of fear

Many experts say that fear microexpression is closely linked to shock, so there are lots of similarities. Make sure you gather enough cluster cues before determining whether someone is fearful or in shock. With fear, eyebrows will raise and draw together, usually in a flat line. Wrinkles will form in the center of the forehead between the eyebrows (not across). The upper eyelid will be raised, but the lower lid should still appear tense and drawn up. You might notice the upper white part of the eye but not the lower white. The person's mouth will likely open to varying degrees (depending on the personality and how the person handles fear), and the lips will either be tense or stretched and drawn back.

Anger

Anger is an emotional state that's typically characterized by feelings of hostility, agitation, frustration, and antagonism towards another. Similar to fear, it can play a part in activating your body's fight or flight response. When feelings of anger stir up, you'll notice the individual becoming very defensive. But that doesn't mean anger is 100% negative. Contrary to what society says, a little anger expressed is much better than suppressed anger. It can be a constructive way for a person to clarify the message they just received from you. Perhaps they are confused or feeling betrayed or hurt by something you're not even aware of. In such a situation, it's better to show their anger so you can quickly read and fix the misunderstanding.

Anger becomes a problem when it's excessive, suppressed for too long, or expressed in unhealthy ways. Abuse, violence, and even diseases like heart attacks are usually the result of uncontrolled anger.

As a general rule, you can spot anger in someone by simply paying attention to a person's body language, physiological responses, facial expressions, paralinguistics, and overall behavior.

Their tone of voice will change, and they may begin speaking gruffly or even yelling. They might even start kicking, hitting, or throwing objects, depending on the degree of anger. You might see them taking a strong stance and choosing to turn away to avoid being confrontational. Their facial expression will mostly be a glare or frown.

Microexpressions for anger:
Did you know that anger is one of the easiest expressions to detect on a person's face? Research conducted by the University of Essex shows that it's the emotion that leaks out the most. It's easy to catch an angry look in someone no matter how much they try to hide it. Lowered eyebrows characterize anger in micro-expressions. Vertical lines generally appear between the eyebrows, and the eyes become turn into a hard bulging stare. The lower lip becomes tense, and nostrils may be dilated. Sometimes the lips can

be pressed firmly together with corners down or in a square shape as if shouting. The lower jaw juts outward. In observation, make sure all three facial areas are engaged before concluding that someone is angry.

Disgust

Disgust is another basic emotion that's part of Ekman's original list. You'll read this emotion in someone by the way they move their body and face. They might physically turn away from the thing disgusting them or even vomit or make the full body gesture that they are about to barf. This sense of revulsion can originate from several things, including unpleasant tastes, sights, or smells. Think of when you opened that box of milk that was sitting in the fridge for two months and how that smell caused you to react. Researchers believe that this emotion evolved as a reaction to foods that might be harmful or fatal. Sometimes we also see this same reaction where there's blood, infection, death, decay, or poor hygiene. Aside from physical factors, people tend to show the same emotion when they feel morally disgusted by something or someone. If the person finds your words or behavior distasteful, immoral, or evil, they might make the same face.

Microexpressions for disgust
You'll see it mainly in the face. The eyes will be narrow, the upper lip raised, and the upper teeth might even be exposed a little. The nose wrinkles up,

and the cheeks are raised, making a very nasty and unattractive face.

Sadness

Sadness is an emotional state we all experience from time to time. Anytime we lost something, failed to attain the desired outcome, or experienced loneliness, sadness came rushing in to join the pity party. It's often characterized by feelings of disappointment, hopelessness, disinterest, grief, and dampened mood. If experienced for prolonged periods of time, it can turn into severe mental health problems such as depression. When observing another, some of the signals you'll spot is withdrawal, lethargy, excessive quietness, crying, and a foul dampened mood. You might also notice drooping eyelids, contracted chest, lowered lips, cheeks, and jaw all sinking downwards from their own weight. That overall sense of heaviness and hopelessness are the cluster signals for sadness.

Microexpressions for sadness
Sadness shows up most clearly in the eye area. The inner corners of the eyebrows will be drawn in and then up, and the skin below the eyebrows will be triangulated with the inner corner pointed upward. The lips also play a significant role because they will be drawn down as the lower lip pouts out. Sadness is one of the most challenging microexpressions to identify correctly. Why? Mainly because sad microexpressions are generally subtle and hard to notice. There is no prominent "tell" sign like a happy

smile because most people don't even like showing sadness. Surprisingly, people can develop a resting sad face (similar to RBF), especially when practiced for prolonged periods.

Aside from these basic emotions, there are other emotions people tend to convey, so it's worth learning what specific signals mean to avoid misinterpretations.

Signs of Interest

How can you tell if someone likes you without downright asking them? Whether you're at a networking event, meeting your new boss, trying to close a client, or eyeballing a potential romantic partner, there are specific verbal and nonverbal signals you can learn to identify to figure it out quickly.

One of the first and easiest to identify is the mirroring technique. What is the mirroring? This is when someone subtly mimics your speech, speech patterns, and non-verbal behavior. People will mirror behaviors when they want to get in sync or harmony with one another. To see this in action, sit at a diner or coffee shop and notice how couples tend to mimic each other's behavior. If you're lucky enough to spot a few people arguing, notice how they seem to do the opposite of mirroring. Even without hearing their argument, you can read that their body language is out of harmony. So, if you want to know how someone feels about you, pay attention to their behavior. Is the person facing you with their entire body? If you're standing or seated, are they mimicking your body posture? Are they copying your vocal volume and cadence? What about their facial expression - does it change to match yours, or does it stay completely flatlined?

Another thing to look out for is how they make eye contact. If their eyes light up with excitement as you speak and they gaze at you for prolonged periods of time, they definitely have an interest. You might also notice that the person is curious, emotionally attentive, or demonstrating some kind of preenish behavior such as straightening their tie or sleeves (if it's a man) or brushing their hair away from their face (both men and women do this).

Signs of Annoyance and irritation

If the person you're reading is annoyed, their tone of voice will be the first giveaway. They might become too loud or too quiet. Annoyance is also evident in the kind of gaze they have. The eyes will either become unnaturally wide or too narrow, and their eye contact may be rigid and prolonged. The lips tend to press tightly together with mounting tension. Overall body posture can also clue you in because most of the time, irritated or annoyed people will be closed, contracted, and stiff with tensed-up muscles.

Signs of Shame

Almost every human displays this universal behavior when they feel ashamed or embarrassed, and it's super easy to spot. When someone experiences shame, there's a natural impulse to slouch downward and touch the side of their forehead. You'll see it even with animations when they try to portray a character as embarrassed. This microexpression lasts a short time but can alert you to what the person is feeling. If the shame runs deep, that forehead touch could turn into a full0on eye block where the person goes from the forehead touch to the eye cover.

Try to observe how a person reacts with both their face and gestures. Watch out for anytime someone touches the side of their forehead or blocks one or both eyes while making an uncomfortable head shake. It could indicate shame or embarrassment, which should inform your next move depending on context and your intentions.

Signs of Confusion or perplexity

Some of the signals you want to look out for are negative microexpressions that come and go. Frowning and downward cast eyes are a good indication that the person is perplexed by something. In some instances, one might touch their chin, forehead, or mouth. We see more "rubbing of the chin or scratching of the head" in men. It could also be characterized by stroking the beard or rubbing the back of the neck.

On the other hand, women tend to pose a finger below the chin or slightly open their mouth and place a finger on their front teeth. You'll also observe the person is having difficulty thinking or speaking clearly, and their emotions may suddenly change to agitation. Their breathing might shift, and heart rate may increase depending on the situation, and it may cause them to start sweating or experience shame, at which point you'll notice the cluster signals for shame. Although it varies depending on the context, confusion can trigger a variety of secondary responses to match their brewing emotional state. If the person has a good temperament and calm personality, the shift may not be so radical, but if you're dealing with an expressive character, they might turn defensive and perhaps a bit hostile toward you.

Microexpressions are going to be vital in helping you decode some of these everyday emotions. Most of the time, people will unconsciously mislead you and try to fake their emotional state. Thanks to micro expressions, you can pick up the truth and interpret the situation more accurately, taking more control of the problem and conversation

Section Four: Tying It All Together

Chapter 11: Understanding People

As human beings, we are not only unique but also quite complex. Even the most straightforward among us has layers upon layers of traits, perceptions, beliefs, qualities, tendencies, quirks, and more. Effective communication becomes almost impossible if we don't develop the aptitude and skillset necessary to read our fellow humans. Whether you are meeting someone for the first time or rekindling a relationship, you will need to develop a personalized framework customized to suit the taste that enables you to understand and read others better.

Thus far, you've been learning bits and pieces of different techniques and strategies for analysis, but without this section, none of what you learned will be of value. Why? Because theory is easier to grasp. Practical applications of speed reading and people analysis require a lot more effort on your part. The intention now is to help you consolidate everything you've learned and share everyday scenarios of what and how to apply your learnings. Let's begin this section by outlining some of the fundamentals you need to know.

First, you should realize that accurately and masterfully reading others will take time and energy.

If you genuinely want to become a masterful communicator, you will need to put in the work. Reading this book is just the beginning and only half the job. The other half is continued practice. When I say practice and give it time, I mean you should be patient with yourself and the person you're interacting with. Decoding someone accurately in sixty seconds or less is possible, but only after decades of mastery. So don't assume that after one quick meeting with someone and a few signals, you've got that person pegged. People are formed of a lifetime of experiences, and like all good things, it takes time and energy to understand a person fully. Refrain from quick judgments and commit to being more open and available to that interaction so you can genuinely get to know someone. If you get stuck in your head for too long, you'll miss the vital data needed for analysis.

The second thing you need to do becomes aware of your biases and assumptions as much as possible. Drop them as soon as you catch yourself making assumptions about another. Try to imagine each person as a blank slate in your mind that you know nothing about until you interact with them and pick up real-time data. That demands your presence. Active listening is one of the critical things you must always do henceforth. If you can stay attentive, mindful, and aware of the person at that moment, you'll pick up far more than any book can teach you on human behavior. Practice mindfulness so you can learn to get fully present. A good exercise you can do to become more mindful is deep breathing. Take a few deep breaths in and out. Notice how the air comes in and goes out of your body. Pay attention to something concrete about the other person to draw you into the present moment. It can be the color of their shirt, the way they move their hands, or whatever captures your attention. Then focus entirely on what they are saying. Really listen as they speak without judgment or the need to argue mentally. If you're struggling with active listening, practice clearing your mind of other things before beginning conversations. When someone speaks to you, focus on what they say, leave a buffer time of silence between their last word and your answer. That will train you to think and reflect before responding.

The last thing I encourage you to do is to get into the habit of asking really good questions. Try to start your conversations with "what" or "how" instead of "why." You should also try to let the other person speak more than you because the more they can reveal about themselves, the more data you'll have for analysis. People tend to avoid engaging too much in "why" type questions because they find it uncomfortable to question themselves, or they could quickly get confused. So opt for "what," e.g., what made you go for that particular choice? That's a much better question than asking, "why did you choose that?"

When we are meeting people for the first time, there are certain things we can take notice of to help us gauge and analyze them faster. Let's go over some of the critical things to put into practice.

Communication styles

Different people communicate differently in any given situation. Although our communication styles might vary under different contexts, e.g., I will carry a different tone with my mom than with my boss, the overall communication style tends to remain constant. That's because communication styles are directly linked to personality traits, and each style has nonverbal cues related to it. By identifying one's communication style accurately, you can pick up a lot of valuable data, including their personality. The main communication styles people subscribe to are assertive, aggressive, passive, and passive-aggressive.

Assertive - Think *"I can't control others, but I can control myself."*

Assertive communication is a style in which individuals state their opinions and feelings and firmly advocate for their rights and needs without violating others.
These individuals are confident, direct, firm, and they value their time and their needs while being very respectful of the rights of others.

An assertive communicator relates to others with sincerity, and they do their best to be authentic,

remain true to themselves while still honoring others. If such a person disagrees with you, they will speak up. In most cases, assertive people exercise plenty of self-control and exhibit emotional stability, making it easy to engage in active communication.
Assertive communicators speak in a calm and clear tone of voice. They actively listen without interrupting others and feel connected to others. Such individuals communicate respect for others and have a relaxed and open body posture.

You'll quickly pick up a person who communicates assertively, even if it's the first encounter. All you need to do is notice how inclusive their body language is (e.g., friendly gaze as you speak, attentiveness, smile, active listening) and how emotionally independent they are. Although they have high confidence, it doesn't come from a place of superiority. Their nonverbal signals reflect calmness and positivity. In conflicts, assertive communicators usually prefer a collaborative approach. They want everyone to give their input and the situation to be resolved in a mutually beneficial way.

Individuals who communicate assertively feel connected to others, are more in control of their lives, and do not allow others to abuse or manipulate them. They have clearly defined boundaries and aren't afraid to stand up for their rights and fight for what they believe in. Experts state that this is the best communication style for any personality type to adopt. It allows us to authentically express ourselves, take care of our own needs, and live by our personal values without disregarding or intruding on others. It gives everyone, including ourselves, the freedom to enjoy a healthy mental, physical, emotional, and spiritually nourishing human experience.

Aggressive - Think, *"I own you."*

Aggressive communication is a style in which individuals express their feelings and opinions and advocate for their needs in a way that violates the rights of others. In other words, they are a bit too much - the extreme of assertiveness. And no one enjoys the company of such a personality.

An aggressive communicator is generally overbearing, critical of others, enjoys humiliating others, and can be very impulsive.

You'll notice how easily offended such a person is even though they treat others in less than empathetic ways. Perhaps the person keeps interrupting you, or they interject and talk louder while you're still expressing your point of view.

These individuals can be extremely annoying, not to mention energy-sucking if you're not careful. This communication style leaves very little room for open communication, and such individuals have no respect for personal boundaries or other people's opinions. The overall tone is harsh, aggressive, judgmental, and often demeaning. You might also notice a lot of vigorous hand movements from the person, and their gaze is generally unfriendly and "cold" in nature. To identify an aggressive communicator, be on the lookout for body cues and negative micro-expressions that disregards your presence. You'll notice an attitude of superiority and importance if you pay close attention. Depending on the degree of aggressiveness, the person might physically invade your personal space or become physical if they feel attacked. Individuals who communicate this way always blame others instead of owning their issues which easily alienates others. They generate strong emotions of fear and hatred in others, and their body posture is quite intimidating and overbearing.

Passive - Think *"People never consider my feelings."*

Passive communication is a style in which the individual has developed a pattern of avoiding expressing their opinions or feelings. This might be to protect themselves from something real or imagined. A passive communicator will use a calm and quiet voice, reserved body gestures, and focus more on listening than talking.

People pleasers tend to fall into this category of communicators. Submissive people also tend to be passive as they too are unable to speak their minds authentically. A defining attribute to the passive style of communication is lengthy silence. Sometimes you might even forget the person is part of the meeting - that's how you know you're dealing with a passive personality type. Ever had one of those?

If you're having a conversation with someone and all they do is agree with you instead of offering their opinion, it could be that they are scared of rejection or coming across as aggressive. To please you, the person may remain silent and periodically nod so they can maintain favor with you. If you get into a misunderstanding with such an individual, they will not directly respond to the hurtful situation. Instead, they will carry that grievance, and over time, minor annoyances will build up into resentment and outbursts. These individuals are not temperamental, but a small trigger can cause a massive eruption, creating damage once they reach their threshold.

Passive communicators often fail to assert themselves, express their feelings, needs, or opinions. They tend to speak softly and apologize for everything. Their body posture is often slumped, and they struggle a lot with direct eye contact. Individuals who communicate through this style often feel depressed, misunderstood, lonely, confused, and struggle with emotions and resentment.

Passive-aggressive - Think *"I'll appear cooperative, but I'm not."*

Passive-aggressive communication is a style in which individuals appear passive on the surface but are really acting out anger in a subtle, indirect way.

This pattern of communication tends to be favored by people who feel powerless, stuck, and incapable. Instead of expressing their anger or directly dealing with their issues, they carry their resentment and find ways (behind-the-scenes) to share that pain and anger. You'll notice that a passive-aggressive communicator uses a lot of sarcasm and hides behind dark jokes. They deny having problems even when you can see them. While a passive-aggressive person might appear collaborative and open to cooperate, they will turn around and do things indirectly to disrupt or even sabotage the very thing they promised to work on.

The problem with this personality type is that you're dealing with someone who doesn't want to acknowledge their anger issues. If you've ever had a colleague or friend who has a problem with you but won't come to you directly to resolve it, then you've likely encountered a passive-aggressive individual. They might mutter words or even gossip with others in your absence, but to your face, they don't say a darn thing! Individuals who communicate through this style tend to remain stuck in positions of powerlessness, becoming a self-fulfilled prophecy. They become alienated from those around them.

There are other subsets of communications styles if you want to dive into finer details, including manipulative communication styles and empathetic communication styles, but by and large, the easiest ones to spot are these four. The key to detecting, analyzing, and interpreting communication styles and personality types fast is to invest more time in understanding yourself. The more time you invest in understanding your attitudes, mannerisms, and emotions, the easier it is to develop empathy. Empathy is the great secret to understanding and handling people better.

Chapter 12: Speed Reading And Analyzing People In The Workplace

Context is everything when reading and analyzing non-verbal communication. Different signals could have different meanings depending on the environment. That's why we need to get a little more specific with the practical applications of your knowledge. We've talked about personality traits, the Enneagram tool, and approaching and interpreting different communication styles. Now let's discuss how you can apply these techniques in the workplace. Depending on your job, you might be dealing with employees only (e.g., IT specialist, procurement, etc.), or you might be customer-facing which means the number of people you come into contact with exponentially increases. Regardless of your current role or whatever role you switch to in the future, handling people is going to be a big part of your day-to-day activities. Finetuning your people skills will be highly beneficial, especially if you want to rise to the top of your field.

Some of the situations that will require people analysis include networking, board room meetings, job interviews, customer services, and so much more. Suppose you attend a work conference that your boss says is mandatory, and he expects you to gather new business contacts. In that case, you'll need to engage in quite a bit of networking, and the best way to connect with and stand out in front of the right people is to employ the techniques learned in this book. Interact with the person in a way that makes them feel good. Be present, observant, and let them do most of the talking. Pay attention to their communication style, movement of their bodies, and the cluster signals they convey. If you notice the person you're interacting with is introverted, you might want to create a comfortable and quiet setting for the conversation. Perhaps you can invite them for lunch or dinner after the conference to get to know them better.

Within the office, you can also observe how your co-workers act and react so you can start handling them in the best way possible. If Robert is an extravert who loves attention and group activities, but Sam is the opposite, try to interact differently. When you want to give Sam some constructive feedback or work with him on something, invite him over somewhere quiet and give him a safe, comfortable space to express himself. Maybe you can even opt to communicate more with Sam on email than constantly walking over to his desk several times a day because you know he doesn't like that. But you can walk over and chat with Robert even in a group setting as much as possible because he gets fuelled by that. When you're dealing with a highly sensitive person, act with them in a way that doesn't offend or irritate them.

You can also use your newly acquired knowledge to persuade and influence people in the workplace. That's an especially critical skill to have if you're in sales. Imagine you're trying to sell a client a product she needs but can't seem to make up her mind. You'll have an easier time getting the close if you can quickly analyze her personality traits, communication style, and body language then persuades her into purchasing with you because you know it's the best solution for her. Identifying her indecisiveness and insecurities can enable you to adjust your language and speak in a manner that reassures her that she's doing the right thing. If you're not in sales, don't worry, persuasion and influence also work on your boss and colleagues to get you more of what you want. If your boss is an assertive communicator, he will appreciate your ability to recognize this. Speak directly, be respectful and focus on communicating the goals you want to achieve and the value you're bringing to the company. If, however, you realize your boss is more of a "feeler" than a thinker, take a different approach. Focus on the vision and ideas abstractly and emphasize creativity instead of tactical and logical solutions.

Let's switch gears for a moment and assume you're the boss or owner of your company. How would you use these techniques to your advantage?

The most obvious answer is in your hiring process. If you can analyze an interviewee and get to uncover their personality traits, attitudes, and values before hiring them, it can save you a lot of heartaches. By reading someone, you can know whether they are the right fit for your business and whether their skills and unique offerings are right for you. This helps you hire the right leaders and employees for your business.

Three techniques that will help you in the workplace:

Technique #1: Pay attention to appearance
Don't get too analytical, but observe what the person is wearing and think about the message they are conveying with their clothing and style. We all know the workplace is a professional environment. When we show up for work or an interview, our clothing is part of our message about who we are and what we stand for. If a man is wearing a power suit, shined shoes, and their hair looks well-groomed, they indicate ambition and confidence. A man wearing Jeans and a T-shirt suggests they prefer to be casual and comfortable. The same goes for women. If a woman wears a suit or an official dress with perfect hair and makeup, that sends a different message to one wearing a tight top with cleavage and a short skirt.

Technique #2: Notice their posture
When analyzing a person's posture, some of the questions you should be asking yourself include: Does this person's posture convey high confidence

or low self-esteem? Notice whether the individual hold's their head high or whether they seem to be slouching. Is the back straight and chest naturally out, or are there signs of an overinflated ego with too much swagger and a puffed-out chest? Both extremes when it comes to body posture (slumped in or puffed out) are tell-tale signs of the personality.

Technique #3: Interpret facial expression paying close attention to microexpressions
People are constantly leaking emotions. You can pick it up in their tone of voice, but you can also see it on their face. Practice deciphering this emotional map by observing subtle facial cues that you've learned in this book. If Sally says everything is in control with a fake smile and you pick up on a negative microexpression that flashes through her face for a moment, you can be certain Sally is drowning in anxiety and confusion. Her clenched jaw and deep frowns suggest she needs more help, and thanks to your ninja reading abilities, you can offer to give more assistance or resources so she can get her job done on time.

The bottom line is this. Reading other people accurately will become an invaluable tool at work. The examples and techniques mentioned in this chapter are but a handful of the more ways and tools that are available to you once you've mastered the basics. Now it's time to start small and build up those analysis muscles.

Exercise:

Consider a few colleagues you can start practicing with. Try to analyze their communication styles and personalities. Observe them for as long as you need, collect the data using the techniques you're learning over the next week. See if it can change your current relations and experience with the chosen individuals. Don't be afraid to personalize these techniques to suit your work environment and current situation. Start small and build on it.

Chapter 13: How To Date Or Befriend People With Complex Personalities

At some point in your life, if it hasn't yet happened, you're going to meet someone that you strongly desire to connect with. Unfortunately, due to differences in personality and communication styles, that connection might come with lots of struggles. Suppose you're an introvert, but you've met a woman you absolutely love who happens to be extroverted. That relationship will have many challenges, and dating may prove impossible if you lack the skills taught in this book. A friend of mine found himself in this very situation a while back. Up until then, he thought it unnecessary to bother about speed reading and effective communication. He never dreamed that he would fancy a girl who was his counter opposite from a personality typing point of view. They struggled to find things that they both enjoyed doing together. Despite their shared feelings of affection and desire to be together, they wanted to call it quits. That's when he came to me for some advice, and I passed on the same suggestions I'm laying out for you. Now, they're engaged and report that things have never been better.

You, like my friend, can learn to handle all personality types and share friendships and companionships with anyone you fancy. But it can only be done when you know yourself better and know how to read and understand other people. Personality differences do not make relationships impossible; they make our relations all the more adventurous.

If you are an extrovert and want to befriend or enter some kind of relationship with an introvert, you need to understand that they need time and space to be alone. Give them the gift of space. Let them recharge, reset and reflect in solitude. Don't take offense when they ask you to stay in over the weekend instead of hitting the clubs. Similarly, if you're an introvert, it should become obvious that an extrovert will need to hit the clubs every weekend, and that's okay. If you don't feel like accompanying them to every social gathering, that is okay. Give yourself permission to decline the invitation, openly let them know you need some alone time, and please allow them the freedom to be social. Only through social interaction and group activities can they reset and recharge. Instead of being overwhelmed by how much they want to be with you and how much activity they wish to engage in, don't interpret that as something negative. View them with empathy and realize that this person simply loves spending time with you and your friends.

Another example we can look at is when you recognize that the person you're with is highly intuitive and loves to engage in creative discussions. Then, by all means, encourage them to talk about their ideas, the future, and where they want to be. It's enough to listen. You don't need to speak if you don't want to. That will naturally cause them to feel valued, loved, and connected to you. If the person is a thinker, perhaps it's best to focus on factual, evidence-based conversations. Don't attempt to force such individuals to discuss their feelings or expect that they will be sentimental. When you want to get an agreement out of them, the best approach is always the one they can best relate with.

Listen and trust your instincts.

Active listening is going to be essential if you want to get along with any personality type. Everyone wants to feel heard, and no connection can occur until the other person feels like you get them. As you listen, don't get too caught up in analysis. Really listen to what the other person is saying, not what you want to say next. Do not follow the urge to reciprocate if you happen to pick up any negative microexpressions or emotions. For instance, if you pick up lots of anger and aggression coming from the other person, resist the natural impulse to raise your voice, point fingers, or speak disrespectfully to the other person. I know that's a challenging task, especially when you feel mistreated, but trust me, the only thing it does is add fuel to the fire.

The more complex the personality, the more you should do your best to use a calm, reassuring voice. If you're engaged with a person who keeps interrupting you and won't shut up, don't react by cutting them off. Instead, wait patiently until the person runs out of breath and then speak your mind.

Simple secrets to getting along with anyone

If you have a co-worker, family relative, or an ex that you try to avoid at all costs because they just press all your buttons, here are a few things you can do to make that experience less unpleasant.

• Work on identifying and taming your triggers.
Remember what we said earlier. The more you understand yourself, the easier it is to understand others and demonstrate empathy. With empathy, you can and will maintain your cool even when engaging with those who rub you the wrong ways.

A huge part of knowing yourself is knowing the subjects and idiosyncrasies that push your buttons. Some people seem to have a master's degree in annoying you. But do you know why they get away with it? Because you haven't invested some time getting to know yourself and why you explode when someone pushes that button. If you could explore what ticks you off and why you'd tame that little sucker and then no one can use it against you. Make your list of triggers (things people like using against you, such as your battle with weight while growing up, politics, etc.). Once you have a list, make a plan for taking control of yourself whenever someone triggers you. Something that works for me is I take deep breaths, and I remove myself at that moment from that conversation. If I can leave the room, then I ask for a short time out. If that's not possible, I mentally zone off and switch to a memory or a thought of someone I love. Whatever allows you to disconnect yourself from the heat of the moment is what I want you to do.

• Resist the temptation to get sucked in.
As soon as you realize you're dealing with a difficult person, don't indulge them. Stop allowing yourself to "have the last word" or even defend yourself. That's precisely what they want so they can keep pushing your buttons even more.

• Use the STOP phrase.
This is a simple technique that seems to work in disarming almost every troublesome person I know. The acronym STOP means **S**orry you feel that way. **T**hat's your opinion, and you're allowed to have it. **O**h, well. **P**erhaps you're right. By speaking these phrases sequentially, the other person will give up trying to suck you into their argument.

Above all else, I want you to realize that no matter how complex or impossible someone's personality is, they are just humans trying to express themselves, even in the most unhealthy ways. Go back and study the Enneagram again and let that inject a little more understanding and empathy when you observe specific behaviors. Most of the time, people are projecting their fears and insecurities when dealing with you. It could be that they are operating at lower levels of their development, and you're interacting with them at their lowest instead of their best. One might feel more secure when they are bullying or trying to control you because, deep down, your presence triggers their insecurities. Maybe they are "acting up" and trying to show you how important they are because they are envious that you're getting a lot of attention. It might even be an issue of belonging whereby the individual plays the victim and uses emotional manipulation to get you to feel sorry for them because they feel lonely and unworthy of love.

Trying to figure out another human being isn't always easy, and it takes time to uncover the unconscious beliefs behind someone's problematic behavior. But that doesn't mean we cannot protect ourselves, tolerate them a bit more, and make that encounter as painless as it can be. Even if we are sure we do not want to nurture a lasting relationship with someone, it's still worth taking some time to read them and develop a framework of understanding and dealing with them at that moment. Most of us assume reading others and effective communication is only used to make friends. Actually, it is used in both positive and negative encounters. Now that you understand how to leverage your communication skills to build rapport and disengage yourself from those that threaten your sanity, I expect you will be calmer, more productive, and more in control of your emotions no matter who you're dealing with.

Chapter 14: Tips For Influencing Anyone

Studies show that we are instinctively wired to imitate the choices of others because we assume that others have the information we don't. And if that other happens to be someone we admire or respect, we assume that missing information they have causes them to make better decisions. So we tend to follow their actions. Combine this knowledge with your people reading skills, and you can practically influence anyone. But what is influence, and can anyone influence another? Influence is the state of social or mental dominance over someone or something. The purpose of influencing another should always be something positive and mutually beneficial. Anyone can influence another, but not everyone does. It requires certain abilities which very few develop. Masterful communication is one of the abilities needed for influence. Have you ever heard of poor communication influencing anyone or changing people's behavior? If anything, the opposite is what we witness in society: a masterful communicator with ill intentions changes the mindset and behaviors of entire populations, leading to things like dictatorship and communism. You can use influence for both good and bad. Choose to use it only for the good of others and yourself. The more you understand how people operate, what makes them tick, and how they feel, the easier it becomes to influence them.

There are many ways to increase your level of influence with the people in your world. A quick and easy hack to get you started is to get into the habit of finding common ground with the person you're interacting with and refraining from attacking their ego with counterarguments. For example, the magazine Wired reported that telling parents who refuse to vaccinate their children that science has shown that vaccines do not cause autism did nothing to alter the parents' behavior. Instead, it was more effective to say that vaccines would protect their children from deadly diseases. This new approach worked because instead of altering people's beliefs and actions by introducing data that was attacking the person's sense of "rightness," they instead focused on offering an argument that did not contract prior beliefs. Instead, it focused on the common goal of keeping children healthy, thus influencing the parents into a new frame of mind that accomplished the desired result. You can take the same approach whenever you're interacting with someone, and they don't seem to be seeing things your way. Rather than force them to come over to your side, learn their communication style and personality, then find common ground so you can "speak their language" and eventually disarm them. Let's take a look at other ways you can quickly influence someone.

Mirroring

Mirroring involves subtly mimicking what the other is doing to establish a sense of connection. The technique involves pacing or matching the person you are trying to lead by mimicking their posture, speech, gestures, and, more importantly, emotions. When pacing is done correctly, you will establish rapport and trust with them, opening them to your ideas and suggestions. In several studies, waitresses, negotiators, and salespeople mirrored their chosen subject's verbal and non-verbal behavior. The outcome of that experiment was quite surprising as the waitresses doubled their tips, negotiators obtained better results, and the store salespeople got greater compliance from customers, ultimately selling more products.

How to mirror someone effectively.

#1: Notice their breathing patterns and synchronize to their breathing
Start by noticing your breathing patterns, then swiftly shift attention to the other person's breathing rate and depth. Look away for a moment, and then check back to see if you're still timed. It takes practice, but the more you do this, the better you'll get.

#2: Match their gestures and posture.
Notice how the person uses and moves their arms. Are the arms folded? What about their posture? Are

they leaning forward and inward? You should too. If the person changes position, wait for a little while and subtly adjust as well. Don't make it too obvious because they will pick it up and get very infuriated if you switch too fast.

#3: Identify the dominant emotion and speech patterns
As soon as you start engaging, pay attention to their tone, volume, and verbal style. Use similar words and phrases. Regularly repeat back some of their words. Do a quick analysis of their emotional state and mimic that with your words and actions.

#4: Shift gears and check for pacing
After some time has elapsed and you feel confident the synchronicity is there. Initiate change on your own, e.g., uncross your arms or lean back. If you've been pacing the conversation correctly, the other person will naturally follow your shift and copy you. That's the signal to step in and take charge.

#5: Begin leading and influencing
Now that you're in charge of the conversation change your emotions to align with your agenda. Start small, paying attention to their shifts along the way. Are their feelings rising to match yours? If you can sense their change in emotions, you're likely to get the outcome you desire. But before making your request or suggestion known, do one last thing. Offer a genuine compliment. Use all the data you've gathered through observation and pick something you genuinely admire or enjoy about them. This act

of praise and appreciation triggers an unconscious need to be more open to you. It's a force multiplier that brings out a greater willingness to follow.

A great example of when you can use mirroring to influence another is while at work. If you're a leader and your team feels emotionally vulnerable, fearful, or frustrated. Follow the steps outlined, match their stress levels at first, get synchronized, then work them into a better state of mind. If you're going in for a job interview, you could use the same process with the interviewer, matching their breathing, using some of the exact phrases they use, matching their posture and emotions. When appropriate, give them a genuine compliment relevant to the present moment and then lead them back into your candidacy with you as the lead. You can also learn to use this with a spouse, a child, or a family member. The only caveat here is that you must always use it with good intentions and for the highest good of all parties involved.

Empathy

The ability to communicate effectively and exhibit empathy will draw people to you and make you influential in people's lives. Empathy has become somewhat of a buzzword, especially in the business community, but it's worth paying attention to it. When you are self-aware enough and capable of identifying, analyzing, and interpreting other people's verbal and non-verbal communication, you already stand out from the crowd because most cannot do that. But if you can take it up a notch and infuse empathy in your approach and interactions with the people you're analyzing, you become a rare gem in our society. Many people are attuned to their own emotions but getting into someone's head is a little trickier. It takes effort and practice to master. How will you gauge and measure your growth as an empathic person?

You'll start to notice that people open up to you more, and they feel safe discussing anything with you. They will often say you're such a great listener. Others will start coming to you for advice, and as your skills advance, you'll quickly detect when someone is lying and when they're honest. As you interact with people, you'll start caring more about how the other person is feeling. These are just a few of the signs that show your empathy is growing.

The more you can exhibit empathy, the easier it will be for people to put down their guards and reveal their true selves to you. That makes it easier to analyze and influence them accurately. Empathy tends to promote helping behaviors. Not only are you more likely to engage in helpful behaviors when you feel empathy for other people, but other people are also more likely to help you when they can feel you're empathetic.

Chris Voss, the master of negotiation and a former FBI hostage negotiator, says empathy is the key to successful negotiation. I would add that it is the key to successful relationships and influence.

How to practice empathy

#1: Work on actively listening to others without interrupting them midway.

#2: Train yourself to agree and respect everyone's opinion even when you don't believe they are right.

#3: Pay close attention to their body language and all the different types of non-verbal cues we've discussed in this book. That includes their paralinguistics.

#4: Be curious and inquisitive. Ask high-quality questions that enable you to learn more about the person, their beliefs, and their lives. That will allow you to understand their frame of mind, and it will help you imagine yourself in their shoes.

Conclusion

By now, one thing should be indisputably clear in your mind. It takes a masterful communicator to read people better. This book has taken you on the initial phase of turning you into a powerful, influential communicator who can handle all kinds of personalities. You've learned the importance of developing speed reading skills and how to begin your practice. In every interaction, you should be engaging your observational skills, paying close attention to the person's verbal and non-verbal messages. And as we said in the earlier chapters, reading and accurately analyzing people requires that you first establish a mental baseline and take in as much data as you can to identify personality cues and communication style.

By figuring out what kind of a person you're dealing with and actively listening to how they use their voice, how they move their bodies and the amount of space they demand to feel comfortable. The eyes, mouth, face, arms, feet, and posture a person holds will communicate various things outlined in the third chapter. But always bear in mind culture and other environmental factors when interpreting the message. As we said, people from different cultures will use different non-verbal cues to convey the same message, and it is upon you to decode their message and transmit something they can understand.

You've also learned some of the main rules to live by when dealing with others and the clues to look out for when dealing with someone manipulative or deceptive. One of the best tools you should take away from this reading is the Enneagram personality typing system. Use it to understand yourself better and to read others faster. With tools like the Enneagram and all the techniques and hacks you learned in section three and four, your ability to remain present, exercise active listening and demonstrate empathy as you emotional intelligence develops should become the natural progression of your skills.

Having come this far, I do not doubt that you're committed to personal growth and that you've got the discipline and sheer determination to seize the opportunities and relationships life has given you. That is just the first step on your journey of masterful communication, and I hope you'll allow this guidebook to catapult you to the next level when it comes to interpersonal relations, both personally and professionally.

With the tools, confidence, and encouragement you've received, I hope you will immediately start practicing everything you've learned. Without practice, you'll never get the full value of this material, and it'll be hard to know just how good you are at connecting, reading, and handling the people in your world. I know for sure that if you continue working on yourself and sharpening your skill set, you will become a better communicator, and this book will have served its purpose.

Now, get out there and start influencing people. All the best!

Resources

Six Tips for Reading Emotions in Text Messages. (n.d.). Greater Good. Retrieved October 7, 2021, from https://greatergood.berkeley.edu/article/item/six_tips_for_reading_emotions_in_text_messages

The Anneberg School of Communications, & Ekman, P. E. (1976). *Movements With Precise Meanings* (26.3). Paul Ekman. http://www.paulekman.com/wp-content/uploads/2013/07/Movements-With-Precise-Meanings.pdf

Toast Masters International. (2011). *Gestures: Your Body Speaks: How to Become Skilled in Nonverbal Communication* (No. 201). Toast Masters Org. https://web.mst.edu/~toast/docs/Gestures.pdf

Thompson, S. (2017, August 25). *Cultural Differences in Body Language to be Aware of*. Virtual Speech. https://virtualspeech.com/blog/cultural-differences-in-body-language

M. (2021, July 19). *Improving Emotional Intelligence (EQ)*. HelpGuide.Org. https://www.helpguide.org/articles/mental-health/emotional-intelligence-eq.htm

Just a moment. . . (n.d.). Patimes.Org. Retrieved October 7, 2021, from https://patimes.org/models-emotional-intelligence/?__cf_chl_managed_tk__=pmd_eWNdTmXBpgfA6AOS9rVHvnSLDixCVlLJJeI5tM4dFE4-1632908638-0-gqNtZGzNAxCjcnBszRNR

Gutiérrez-Cobo, M. J. (n.d.). *The Three Models of Emotional Intelligence and Performance in a Hot and Cool go/no-go Task in Undergraduate Students.* Frontiers. Retrieved October 7, 2021, from https://www.frontiersin.org/articles/10.3389/fnbeh.2017.00033/full

The Enneagram Personality Test. (2021, October 4). Truity. https://www.truity.com/test/enneagram-personality-test

Paler, J. (2021, August 22). *How to read people like a pro: 17 tricks from psychology.* Hack Spirit. https://hackspirit.com/how-to-read-people/

Bariso, J. (2021, January 5). *An FBI Agent Shares 9 Secrets to Reading People.* Inc.Com. https://www.inc.com/justin-bariso/an-fbi-agents-9-ways-to-read-people.html

Milton Keynes UK
Ingram Content Group UK Ltd.
UKHW021834041223
433765UK00021B/2017